Copyright © 2019 by Jacob Asplund

All rights reserved. This book or any portion thereof
may not be reproduced or used in any manner whatsoever
without the express written permission of the publisher
except for the use of brief quotations in a book review.

Published in the United States of America

First Printing, 2019

Paperback
ISBN 978-1-7337895-0-9

EPUB
ISBN 978-1-7337895-1-6

My Journey with God

by Mary Lee Reuss

Table of Contents

Introduction 1
Family History 3
My Early Years with Grandma
 and Grandpa Lee 12
Hagerstown 15
School Experiences 26
The Neighborhood Gang 30
Berkeley Springs 41
Paxtang 49
Brookeville 52
Brookeville Society 56
Sarah's Story 67
Niagara Falls 72
Bryn Mawr 82
Baltimore 88
El Paso 97
Clarksville 101
Back in Bryn Mawr 104
Richmond 109
A Trip to Columbus 115
Cape May 116
Richmond Again 118
Hapeville 119
Return to Richmond 121
Valparaiso 123
Working in Valparaiso 129
Janesville 132

Summer Fairs 138
Goat Dairy 140
My Career as a Nurse 145
Training Resumes 149
Mendota 151
Public Health Nursing 155
Community Programs 166
Caravilla 170
Rock County Mental Hospital
 173
Foster Children 174
Family Trips 177
Skaalen Home 190
Leaving Janesville 192
Arizona 194
Stoughton 199
Return to Arizona 202
My Husband 203
My Children 209
Fred 214
Tom 216
Linda 217
Martha 219
Noah's Ark Trip 220
In Conclusion 222

Introduction

I will take you with me on my journey through 95 years of adventures as God revealed His plan for my life.

It begins with the adventures that brought my immediate ancestors through their tribulations. It continues with my own survival from a typhoid epidemic, nurturing at first, then childhood experiences, then learning to survive, encounters with death as a child, abandonment, rescue, encounters with death as a teen, maturing, nurses training cut short, marriage, childbirth, rescue of a child, career fulfillment, and encounters with death as an adult. There are experiences with floods, tornados, a downdraft, and a small tsunami. There are trips to Mexico, Alaska, Holland, Germany, France, Switzerland, and Hawaii.

God met me as a child of 6 in Sunday School, He continues to be with me as a real God that I can depend on. He brought my parents back into my life as a teen and an adult and taught me to understand, appreciate, forgive, and love them as they were. He gave me many opportunities to use the gifts He gave me to love, help and serve others through my nursing, community service and care of 22 foster children. He gives me "wake up calls" when I am careless and "coincidences" to remind me that He is everywhere all the time.

As a result of this focus on my time as a nurse and foster mother, I have not included some details and occurrences because of privacy concerns. However, I will record the many lessons I learned from them in the situations God put me in.

I will also include a story about Sarah that I wrote for credit in English.

I hope you will look back on your life, see God at work, and pass it on to your family and friends.

He loves you!

Family History

I know more stories about my mother's side of the family, so I will start with them. I will tell stories about my father's side when I tell about living in Brookeville with Aunt Verdie.

My mother was Margaretta Stuart Lee. Her father was James Eugene Lee and her mother was Verna Imogene Parsons. The Lees and Parsons came over from England before the revolution.

My father was Stanley Dorsey Owings. His father was Henry Howard Owings and his mother was Elizabeth Dorsey. The Owings family came over from Wales with Lord Calvert before the revolution. The Lees, Parsons, Dorseys and Owings families fought in the Revolution, so I am a Daughters of the American Revolution member.

Grandma Lee told me about a Dr. Parsons who lived in New York City. At that time there was a smallpox epidemic in the world. If it was known that some passengers had it, they were not allowed to land. The ship stayed in the harbor until the authorities thought they were all dead. Then they burned the ship. Dr. Parsons told them that some people had lived through the epidemic in Europe, so it was wrong to kill them. He got permission to make a floating raft and take food to the people on the ship as long as they came, and when all the sick people had died, then the ship was allowed to land. He received an award from the city, as many were saved before the epidemic was over.

This story was important to me because I had the certificate given to me by grandma. At that time we were living in Janesville with no medical insurance. Fred had been sick and then he had a stroke so we had bills we couldn't pay to Dr. Herbert Snodgrass. He took the certificate as payment and said he would take it to the medical society museum in Madison.

My great grandmother was Margaretta Stuart Lee. She came from France. Her father was a doctor in France where her mother died. Her father placed her in an orphanage there and came to Detroit to practice. He brought her to Canada and placed her in an orphanage there where he could see her often. He became ill, and asked a friend of his, a Dr. Lee to marry her because he wanted her to be cared for. She was seventeen. The first time she saw her husband was on her wedding day. He was quite a bit older than she was. They had two sons, Floyd and my grandpa James.

Because her husband wanted her to be able to support herself when he died, he placed her in a nursing school and she became a midwife. She worked until she broke her hip at 93. I knew her and will tell you more about her later.

She took in an Irish immigrant 15-year old girl who had been raped by her employer and put out on the street. She delivered the baby and placed them in a Christian home. Because she had the two teenage boys living with her and her husband had died, the church that she belonged to at that time made my grandmother and her two children stand up in front the congregation and excommunicated them – because she had allowed her two sons to associate with a woman of "ill repute". That meant a lot to my grandfather because he believed that he could not go to church – and he never did again. His brother married a Catholic lady and joined that church. Great Grandmother, however, said, "God gave man the power to say who could go the church, but no man is keeping me out of heaven!" She read her Bible and I am sure that she is in heaven today.

My great grandma Parsons was born in born in Buffalo, New York. She married my great grandfather who worked in a factory there. She was a member of the Women's Christian Temperance Union. One winter my great grandpa came home wearing his big heavy overcoat. For a joke, someone had put an empty bottle of whiskey into his pocket without his realizing it. He hung his coat up by the fireplace and Great Grandma found the whiskey bottle. She got her two children, my grandma Verma and her brother Seymour, out of bed that night and took them to her family, asking her father to take them in. Her father said, "No, you are married. Turn right around with your children and go home!" The next morning she and her children left their home and started on foot on a journey that took them to Wichita, Kansas. Along the way she stopped at farm houses and taught people to read, write and cipher in exchange for room and board.

My grandmother Verma's childhood memory includes getting a piano from people who were going west. Their wagon had broken down and the piano was too heavy so they sold it to my great grandma. Great Grandma made my grandma sit by the hour with a board up her back to make sure she sat up straight doing the scales over and over. She hit my grandma on the hands with a ruler if she didn't hold her hands correctly. Grandma had to play perfectly so that she could be an example to bring in music students for her mother. Grandma eventually became a concert pianist in Detroit when she lived with her mother. However, when she married she made her husband promise her she would never have to play again.

They lived on the outskirts of Wichita, next to Indian territory. Because of the danger, the sheriff taught Great Grandma how to shoot a pistol and told her to fire it if she needed help. One night they were coming home from a prayer meeting and saw drunken Indians in their living room through the window. Great grandma told Seymour to go to the kitchen and bring her the broom inside the back door. He said, "OK, Momma. You going to use a broom? Why not the pistol?"

"Get the broom!" she ordered and she chased them out with that broom! My grandma said she would never forget how scared she was, hanging on to her little brother.

Grandma remembers cowboys driving through the streets and filling the bars. Decent people stayed home until they left. The streets were mud and when they walked on the boardwalk she had to hold on to her mother's skirt while Great Grandma made the men get out of her way. I took grandma to a cowboy movie once and she said the scenes were ok, but the cowboys weren't that good. She liked Jesse James, though, because he helped people.

Great Grandma heard that her husband had died on a cattle drive. She was told that he had been killed by Indians, but that was not true. He had tried to follow his wife and children but lost them. On the way, he took a job on a ranch driving cattle to market. On a cattle drive, they were attacked by Ogalala Sioux Indians. He was injured and left for dead, but he had rescued the son of the Chief, so the Indians rescued him and adopted him into the tribe. He had heard that his wife and children had died, so he married a squaw and had a child. When the war was over, he was put in jail so he would not be able to follow his Ogalala family on their forced march west to a reservation. Many died on the journey and my great grandpa never found out what became of them. After being released from jail, he got a job in Detroit as a shopkeeper. My Grandfather Lee found him many years later, old and sick, and brought him home to live with him in York until he died. I was a baby then and he died before I was two.

Great Grandma decided to move to Detroit because oil had been discovered in Indian Territory and the Wichita area had become too rowdy to bring her children up in. She bought a rooming house and put Grandma to work. Grandma earned money playing piano in the orchestra and writing out bills for businesses. One day, when delivering the bills downtown, she saw a typewriter in a window with a sign that said the owner would teach someone to use it and then would give them a job. She signed up. Her mother told her that it was not a proper job for a young lady living in her boarding house. Grandma left home and went to live in another boarding house that was near.

On her birthday, Great Grandma invited Grandma to her birthday party to play the piano and she agreed. She also invited Grandpa James Eugene Lee, who lived in a boarding house across the street, because he played the violin. With Great Grandma's permission, he invited Great Grandpa Springstein, who lived across the hall from him, as he played a mouth organ. The stage was set – Grandma met Grandpa and Great Grandma met Great Grandpa!

Great Grandpa Springstein was born in New York City. His family decided to join a wagon train headed for the west. They gave some money to the wagon train leader and promised to work off the rest when they got to their destination. A disease broke out and only his six-year old sister and he were left of his family. When the train got near where Chicago is now, the train leader sold him and his sister to a family who were clearing land. He promised to work for them and clear land as long as they did not sell his sister. They agreed and he went to clear land a day's journey away. When he returned, he found that they had sold her. He ran away and followed the wagon train with his sister as it headed south. He traced her to St. Louis, but she was shuffled to a new train to be sent farther west and he was unable to find her.

The civil war had begun and he was a runaway indentured servant, so he headed north and joined the Union Army. He was sent east where he got a leg wound. He lost the leg below the knee. He found his way to Detroit where he was a storekeeper when Great Grandma found him. After they were married, they lived in Detroit until they were old and needed help. Then Grandpa Lee moved them to live with him in York.

When the Spanish American war broke out, Grandpa Lee joined the army because he was in the National Guard. Grandma did not want him to go, but married him when he came home. They continued to live in Detroit. Grandpa worked with Henry Ford as fellow workers. He bought a car, but left it home when he went on a business trip on a train. He called Grandma and told her he would take a cab home from the train station. She decided to drive the car to meet him. She had never driven, but thought she knew how. No license was needed then. She did fine until she got to the station. There was a round road in front of the station with a watering pool for horses in the middle. Pandemonium broke loose as she drove up and didn't know how to stop the car! Grandpa jumped on the running board after she had circled around the watering pool several times and stopped the car. She never drove again!

My mother, Margaretta, was their first child. When Grandma was eight and a half months pregnant, she was on her knees cleaning the floor when she got her first contraction. She crawled to the bedroom, climbed onto the bed and held on to the bars at the head of the bed. The contractions came very hard. She heard the knock on the front door and yelled. The door burst open – Great Grandma Lee rushed in, looked at her, ran to the bathroom rolling up her sleeves, ran back, put her fingers in the baby's mouth, pulled down, and delivered the baby. The baby's head had been caught on her mother's pelvic bone. Great Grandma Lee breathed into the baby's mouth, cleaned out mucus, turned her over, and slapped her on the back – then the baby cried. Then she cut the cord and handed her to Grandma. She told Grandma that God had given her a dream to come right away even though the baby was not due for two weeks. My mother was named after her – Margaretta Stuart Lee.

My mother was called Peggy. She was very imaginative – a favorite of her father and a puzzle to her mother. She was a gifted artist, drawing charcoal portraits of many people for fun and income. As a child she pretended to be other people or animals for days at a time, Grandma said. The family moved to York and her sister Virginia was born five years later. As a teen, my mother rebelled, cut her long hair, wore makeup and short dresses, smoked, and drank liquor. She met my father at a party. He had rebelled against his parents, too. Both sets of parents objected, so they eloped. They lived in an apartment in another town where my father worked. When my mother became pregnant and sick, she came home, delivered me, nursed me, weaned me, and went back to my father. She did the same with my brother Jim.

My dad was raised in a Christian home. All the family and their slaves attended a small Christian church. He had six brothers and two sisters. He told me that his father whipped the seven boys every night at the dinner table. Each boy had to confess each sin he had committed that day. If he couldn't think of any they got whipped twice with a buggy whip. The two girls had to watch as their punishment. The whippings ended when the boys were able to take the whip away from their father. After supper their mother would take them into the living room and tell them Bible stories about love and Jesus. Their father was stern with them and taught them good behavior at home and in church.

Now I know why my father tied my brother up to the bathroom door and whipped him when he was naughty and made me watch, he was imitating his father. He whipped me on my legs when I was naughty, but otherwise he was nice when he was sober.

All the children got scarlet fever except my father and his brother Jim. They were the two youngest of the children. They were sent away to relatives so they wouldn't get scarlet fever, therefore they didn't see the gentler side of their father taking care of the boys that got sick. He fed, bathed, and took care of them until they survived. He hired a teacher that came and lived with them until they were old enough to go away to school for the seventh grade.

When my father went away to school, he told about how grandpa took and left him at a cross-road. He said his father pointed out two farms that his older sons had worked for, gave him his choice and said "I want you to go and find yourself some work. Take these letters with you. I will give you a good recommendation and so will your older brothers but you will have to find a place to work." And my father did. He graduated from high school when he was 14 but even though he was a genius in math they didn't recognize it back then. When I lived Brookeville, later, I went to that high school and saw a plaque with Dad's name and Sarah Chitchester honoring them.

My Early Years with Grandma and Grandpa Lee

Great Grandmother delivered me, but my mother went to the hospital to deliver my brother Jim where she dislocated her hip which caused her trouble ever after. While Great Grandma Lee was there, a typhoid epidemic broke out that killed thousands of people. Babies got it and then whole families. They found out that a man who put caps on the milk bottles was a carrier. I contracted the disease. The family doctor came to the house and told my grandma that they could not save babies. She was to take my body and wrap it in a blanket or sheet and put it in a wagon that would come down the street every day. The driver would ring a bell. Then she was to call him because he had to keep a record and give it to the people who would put my name on the wall by the mass grave outside the city.

Great Grandma heard him and told Grandma that maybe the doctor couldn't save babies, but she could if God willed. When she was in Detroit there had been an epidemic. That experience taught her how to take care of me. She took me to a room above the kitchen and boiled, burned or buried everything that came out of the room. No one else in the family got it and I lived. The doctor came and scolded Grandma for not notifying him when I died. She told him to look in the other room. He said "You kept the body," I was playing on the floor, fever free but with boils on my bottom. He asked Great Grandma "How can this be? You didn't tell me you knew how to cure this." She told him he didn't ask her.

My grandma was a very independent little lady, she didn't have any friends. She said that we were to be friendly to neighbors – that was all that was required. I never heard her mention God or read the Bible. Grandpa was only home at night and some Sundays as he was part owner of a paper manufacturing plant. He read his Bible and taught me to pray "Now I lay me down to sleep. I pray thee Lord my soul to keep. If I die before I wake, I pray thee Lord, my soul to take. If I should live for other days, I pray thee Lord to guide my ways." Sometimes he gave me a bath and put me to bed.

I spent very little time with my brother because he had polio. I saw him at supper and played dominoes with him when he could. Christmas was Santa Claus and Easter was the Easter Bunny.

At the time Jim and I were under five, the people living with us were our grandparents, Aunt Virginia, who married and moved away, and Great Grandpa Springstein. Great Grandma Springstein moved to her room and stayed there after Grandpa Lee brought Great Grandpa Parsons home. She said she was a sinner to have married when her husband was still living. Grandma waited on her till she died. Both of my great grandpas liked one another. Then Great Grandpa Parsons died. I don't remember either of them, but Great Grandpa Springstein told me the stories Great Grandpa Parsons had told him about living with the Indians. Later I read children's stories about indian children that reminded me of those stories.

I remember a lot about Great Grandpa Springstein because I was turned over to him when Jim got Polio. If I was good, I was allowed to watch him put on his wooden leg. He had built himself a custom foot. Using a strap that went up through a hole in his pocket, he could move the toes up and down. The heel stayed solid on the ground. He also made his own false teeth. White teeth for normal, black teeth for chewing. We loved to see them at supper against his white mustache! He carved them of wood and used white and black buttons for teeth. He used with red sealing wax to make them waterproof. He carved other things of wood, too that hung on the wall.

He taught me to read by using his cough medicine "hexylresorcinol" and a dictionary. I got pennies for making words and used those pennies to buy candy at the store. I had to wait until he asked me what I wanted, then I had to figure out how many pennies I needed. One lady pinched some fruit and Great Grandpa told her she was stealing. She got mad and left. I was surprised that the storekeeper thanked him. She ruined the fruit and it has to be thrown away, the storekeeper told me.

I could read when I was four, my first book was <u>The Little Dutch Twins</u>. Then Great Grandpa had me find words in the newspaper. I also had to know the meaning of all the words I learned. He taught me to bargain with the farmers who came with wagons to sell meat, fruit, and vegetables. I got to ride the horse that pulled the wagon sometimes. The first time, we reached a corner there was a water tub for the horse and I almost fell in, but Great Grandpa caught my dress! We took long walks while he told me stories about the nature around us. I had only one other girl to play with – my cousin Genevieve – but I seldom saw her.

I was sent upstairs to call Great Grandpa Springstein one morning for breakfast and found him at peace. His hands were folded on his open Bible with the overhead bed light shining on his face. He had died. Later, I had to climb up steps to the coffin in the living room to kiss his cheek. It was so cold. Grandpa assured me he was in heaven that night when I said my prayers. I didn't want to finish them with "…and if I should die before I wake…" He told me that God had a lot for me to do before He took me to heaven – so I finished praying.

The night I left home my grandma said that my parents were coming to take me to live with them. I asked who they were and she said, "The people that give you presents at Christmas." When they came, my father picked me up to hug me, but his cigarette burned my eyelid so they took me to the doctor's house for treatment. After treating me and covering my eye he said only the lid was hurt. Jim was not coming because he still needed the doctor's care. I cried as we drove away and then fell asleep. When I woke, we were at our house and I was introduced to Mrs. Moats, who was to be my caretaker. I came to love her.

Hagerstown

A description of my home follows: I was told that it was the former brick mansion of the founder of Hagerstown. It had been converted into a duplex. The Long family lived on the other side of the duplex, and we seldom saw them. It was located at the top of the hill at 181 South Prospect Street. We had a large front porch next to the side walk. It was a four-story home with a basement that extended to an open area behind the house because it was built in to the hill.

The entrance faced a curving staircase, to the left was a hall way that led to the kitchen, and to the right was the reception room. In the reception room was a fire place above which was the portrait of great-grandpa Springsteen that I gave to my daughter Martha. Through the double doors was a living room with an alcove where my mother drew portraits for people. The living room opened through to the dining room with a door into the kitchen which was in the back of the house. There was a pantry off of the kitchen which had a stairway that led to the second floor. There was also a doorway from the kitchen at the back of the house which opened onto a porch that extended across the back of both apartments.

Upstairs there was a large front bedroom with a powder room, a middle large bedroom, and a third large bedroom that my brother and I used. Down the hallway past the bedroom was a large bathroom. There was a large porch extending from our bedroom to the back of the house which had a door to the bathroom. There was also an outside staircase that led to the back yard. Farther upstairs in the attic there were two bedrooms, a living room, a bathroom, and a large storage room. That is where Mrs. Moats and her little boy, Edgar, lived. The basement was very interesting. There was a large walk in fire place, several storage rooms, a laundry room, and door to a large court yard.

The backyard had three terraces. The first had a patio and a flower garden. The middle terrace also had a flower garden and a row of large trees at the top of a hill. The lower terrace had a fish pond with plants growing in it, as well as the fish. It was by the road, and the garage was located there on a road that extended from the street at the top of the hill to the road below. Beyond the road, at the bottom, there was a swamp. Above the swamp, there was a hill at the top of which were the B&O Railroad tracks. On the other side of the train tracks was the lime quarry.

We were forbidden to play in the swamp because of quicksand. We didn't know what that was, so we played there anyway until a little dog followed us one day and fell in, and we couldn't get him out. We had been playing Tarzan, swinging on a rope over the top of the quicksand. We were very careful after that, but still played in the swamp.

We had a dog named Chico, which means "little boy" in Spanish. He was a German Shepard. If they sent him for us when we were playing, we had to come home. He would herd us and nip our little fingers to make us go home. One time we came home from school, and the roof of the house and the fourth floor were on fire. Someone yelled, "Kids, kids, you have to get the kittens away from the dog. He's eating them!" Well, he wasn't. He was carrying the kittens out in his mouth, and dropping them under the bush. The mother was carrying kittens too, by the neck. They saved five kittens. His fur and the cat's fur was singed. The house was saved, and a lot of repair work had to be done on the roof. It was a brick house. They didn't thoroughly repair the top floor, as we didn't have a maid then.

Our dog Chico also rescued a little boy from the lake. The lake froze over but around the edges of the lake were springs, so the ice would be soft there. The little boy toddled out onto the lake. Men couldn't get to him right away because the ice was too thin. Chico crawled out on his belly, caught hold of the little boy's jacket, and held his head up until the fireman could get a long ladder to lie on the ice to rescue him. Chico had his picture taken and put in the newspaper. We showed this picture off at school.

When we were younger, six or seven, beef cattle were driven right through the streets. They would load the cattle into the boxcars right at the base of the street on the B&O Railroad. That was a lot of fun. We had to get out of the way because the cattle would come right up on the porches. Sometimes they would herd other animals. Once in a while, pigs, but not often.

This was during the Recession in the 1930's, a lot of people and families traveled on the railroad in empty cars without being arrested. There were shacks and tents in the swamp where they stayed. They went from house to house begging for food and offering to work. They put markings on the fence gates of homes to indicate that the people who lived there would feed them. That's when I saw people eat with a sharp knife for the first time. Our maid always made mashed potatoes so they could put other food with it and getting it in their mouths without cutting themselves. That was fascinating to me. My parents were very generous at that time. They fed families and people that were homeless, sometimes my mother would let the maid give the children baths and sometimes I got to help. There was always a turn over as these people searched for work. Once there was a young boy that mother called "Little Man" that we took into our home for a month or two, while his father worked for a neighbor. Mother drew a picture of him. He taught us some naughty words for which our mouths were washed out with soap. Lesson learned. Then he moved on.

Mother was an artist and an actress. I remember one play she was in. It was called ***Broomsticks Amen***. It was a Pennsylvania Dutch play. She was in a lot of other plays too. She loved to draw charcoal portraits of people in the alcove off the living room and had many people pay her to do so. I have some of her portraits and have given some to my children. She left our care to Mrs. Moats at first, then other maids, then finally, in fifth grade, we were on our own.

My father was a partner in the Keller Stonebreaker Insurance Agency and he did very well at first. We had money, and he would play with us and read the funny papers, too but he would become abusive when he started drinking. My father did have knowledge of God and Jesus but Christmas was Santa Claus, and Easter was the Easter Bunny.

My parents were members of the Country Club and had many friends who had parties there. They loved to dance and go out in the evening. Jim and I learned to putt on the children's putting green.

We also got to visit the farm with the ponies for playing polo at a friend of my parents'. Our family doctor, Dr. Fred Miller, was a special friend. Having money was not a problem until Dad became an alcoholic. Mother was allergic to alcohol, but did not realize it until many years later. She could get drunk on very little alcohol. She did not crave it, but social drinking was the style then and she suffered the consequences.

One Sunday, when I was first in Hagerstown, I saw some children walking by the house one Sunday morning with their parents. They told me they were going to Sunday school at a church on the corner. I asked if I could go and they said they would take me if my mother said so. I ran and asked Mrs. Moats and she gave permission after mother agreed. It was at that Protestant Episcopal Sunday school that I first heard about Jesus and His love for me. I knew God loved me, and now I knew His Son did, too! I went regularly after that. My brother came to live with us the next year and went too.

One Sunday he said "What do they do in that big building?" It was the church. Our building was separate. He had seen parents taking their children from Sunday school to church. "Do we have to have a grown up take us?" he asked. "No, you can go by yourself" the teacher said. So we went.

We walked all the way to the front, but all the doors to the pews were shut. We looked at the altar and saw the most unusual altar I have ever seen. From ceiling to floor, the back wall was covered with a story of the creation to the resurrection in brass. The bottom scene was Adam and Eve in the garden, next was the baby Jesus with Mary and Joseph, then the crucifixion, and finally, the Ascension!

We turned around from the altar thinking there was no room for us, then we saw people in the balcony waving to us to come up. As we started down the aisle, a little old lady dressed in black opened the door to her pew and tapped my brother with her black cane that had a silver lion's head on it. She motioned to us to come in. It had a thick red cushion to sit on. She had a black instrument in her ear, so we knew she did not hear well. We sat in that pew every Sunday we were able until we left. We did not have money to put in the black bag that was passed on a pole often, so we put pretty stones if we found some. No one ever said anything! I do not remember anything the pastor preached, but he had white hair that changed colors as he moved due to the sun shining through the stained-glass windows.

The following story illustrates the story of the beginning of our faith in God, which sustained us throughout our lives.

When I was ten and Jim was nine, we had little supervision. One Saturday, Jim and I walked across the road, through the swamp and climbed the bank where the railroad tracks were. There was a large, black oil tanker sitting empty on a siding. Jim decided to investigate. As he looked down inside the tanker, he thought he saw something move inside and started to climb down on old iron rungs inside. He fell into the water and oil in the bottom. I tried to rescue him and fell in too!

Jim started to cry "No one knows we're here! We're going to die!" I said "God knows where we are. He'll help us!" "I can't see Him," Jim yelled. "Neither can I," I said. "But the Sunday school teacher said He's everywhere. He'll come." We both yelled, but no one came. I said the school teacher told me that we could get help by banging SOS (Save Our Souls). We practiced this on our desks at school. Luckily, I had the broken iron rung in my fist from when I fell. I began to bang on the side of the tanker with the iron rung.

BANG! BANG! BANG! BANG! ... BANG! ... BANG! ... BANG! BANG! BANG!

Suddenly, a dirty tramp's face appeared in the opening of the tanker. "What are you two doing down there?" he said. "I'll help you out!" His rope belt was too short, so he went away to get some vines from the swamp to tie on it and pulled us out. Jim cut his leg on the broken ladder and I was trying to get him to stop crying when I looked around to thank the tramp. But he had disappeared – we could see up and down the tracks and on either side of the bank where the tracks were, but saw no sign of him. Jim said that the Sunday school teacher told him that angels could take the form of people. Abraham had men visit him and he even fed them. They were angels! So we decided that God had sent an angel! That was the first time that a homeless man had saved me.

We got whipped of course when we got home, because we ripped our clothes and our shoes had to be thrown away. But we did tell our parents about the tramp angel. Our dad looked at us kind of funny and he said, "You know, that's possible."

When I was ten, I was sent to a camp in the summer for two weeks. One night, I had a severe belly ache with fever and vomiting. An intern arrived and gave me castor oil. The next afternoon, our family doctor came to visit me. When I told him how I had had such a bad belly ache, the nasty medicine and diarrhea but felt better after a terrible pain, he picked me up and carried me to his car, yelling for the intern.

On the way to the hospital, he scolded the intern and said I would probably die as my appendix had ruptured and all be could do was try to operate, sew me up and pray the infection didn't kill me. I was terrified, and begged him to baptize me. He was so sorry he had forgotten I was listening and promised to baptize me if I was going to die. I felt better, as I trusted him and knew I believed in Jesus and would be saved if I was baptized. Because I had heard the pastor say so. I spent the rest of the summer as an invalid – fevers and chills – with frequent visits from the doctor to open and drain the incision, until by September, I was able to go to school. Doctor Fred came to the camp just in time!

After Mrs. Moats left to get married, an older lady named Sue took her place. We did not like her because she insisted on giving us baths together and washing us herself! She took us to her church one evening. The people yelled and fell on the floor as the pastor screamed about demon rum and tobacco! We were frightened as Sue joined them in yelling. We knew our parents smoked and drank alcohol, of course. When we were in bed that night my little brother said, "I don't want to go to heaven with those people!" Neither did

I, so we decided to go downstairs and drink some of the highballs that were left in the glasses from our parents before they went to the country club. We rolled cigarette stubs in newspaper and then lit them, too. Our noses got burned.

The next day we went to our own Sunday school. When the teachers wanted to know how our noses got burned, we told them and then we cried, "We don't want to go to hell, either, and get all burned up!"

The teacher said "The Bible doesn't say that you have to scream and yell and lay on the floor. I don't think you have to. You do need to obey the Ten Commandments and be sorry if you make a mistake and tell Jesus. Then He forgives you and you can go to heaven. He says you must not drink too much, either. There is not anything about cigarettes in the Bible. You were naughty to drink the highballs, because they weren't yours. That is stealing. Will you tell Jesus that you are sorry?"

"Yes, we won't ever do that or burn our noses again," I said and Jim nodded his head. "Then you will go to heaven with Jesus," she said. We felt better about our parents, too.

Sue left after a year, then we had people take care of us when our parents were on trips or stayed with friends. Once a black girl named Rosie came for several days. There was a lightning storm. She got frightened and took us to her house. We had fun playing with the black children after the storm, running barefoot in the street and sailing paper boats in the gutter. When mother came home I told her that Rosie had a picture of Jesus that showed him as a black man. She didn't come again. There was also a black man from the hotel who came to look in on us.

The B&O railroad brought a box car with a whale preserved in formaldehyde and placed it on a siding near the foot of our hill at the height of the evolution debate in our city. In Sunday school, the teacher said that we must believe the story of Jonah in the Bible is true. Jim and I decided to see the whale.

We paid twenty-five cents. The odor was awful and made our eyes tear up. The whale's mouth was held open with a board and there was an apple in its throat. This was to show how small it was. When we got out, Jim said, "Maybe that whale couldn't swallow Jonah, but God made one that did!" Yes, He did!

Years later, a man came to Chicago that had been swallowed by a whale off the coast of Australia. He was blind and his skin was burned, but he was all right otherwise. The whale had been harpooned, but the sailor fell overboard as he struggled and the whale swallowed him. The whale was towed behind the ship until morning when it was hauled up onto the ship. When the other sailors started cutting into the whale to harvest the blubber, the swallowed man fell out. He was taken to Sydney to the hospital. The Salvation Army brought him to Chicago for us to see. He was going to England later.

Scientists said that the whale was old and its digestive juices were weak. It was probably going to die and drift to the shore. Old whales often vomited, too, as they could not digest their food. Indians gathered the vomit as it floated on the water and used it for medicine. There are places in California and Australia and other islands where whales wash up when they die.

School Experiences

My first year of school was a private kindergarten – I remember little of it except that I had a collapsible metal cup. My first grade was at the elementary school down the hill to the south, around the circle by the lake, and about two or three blocks up a slight hill by the park, and across the street. There was a playground for the boys and one for the girls. The school was a red brick three story building on a hill. My first grade teacher was Miss Morning. She had long black hair that she sometimes let the girls braid. In the morning, we stood by our desks and said, "Good morning Miss Morning!" Sometimes giggling, then recited the Pledge of Allegiance, before beginning our day.

From the time I was in first grade until I graduated from sixth grade, school became a safe haven for me and Jim. An alternate route to school was to take the path by the lake through the park. Many times in the spring I choose that path to watch the swans teach their signets to swim. They let them climb on their back, then they swam out on the lake. Then they reached around and threw them one by one into the lake. How they peeped and swam back to their mother or father, as the parents swam away! At last they were allowed to climb aboard again! By this time the school bell had rung, and I was late. I had to stand in the corner until recess. I got a spanking at home when Jim told on me. But it was worth it.

Jim came to live with us the summer before I was in second grade. And our life together really began then. He was a curious little boy – gifted even then with mathematical abilities. He wanted to explore everything, and followed the leadership of the other boys in our gang. They used to give him their math problems, and he did them in his head to their amazement.

Later his third grade teacher, Mrs. Eisenmonger, did not appreciate him. I had to stay after school one day and wait in the cloak room for him to go home with me. I heard her yelling at him, "Show me how you got the answer!" He yelled back, "I see it in my head, it is right!" Next, I heard a thump and a scream. I ran into the room to find Jim holding his head, and the blackboard broken. The teacher was holding him and shaking him – he began to cry. She yelled, "I am taking you home." She walked us all the way home, knocked on the door, and said, "He's too stupid to teach." She turned around and stormed off down the street. Jim had a big knot on his forehead, his nose began to bleed, and he complained that he was sick to his stomach.

Mother called our family doctor, Dr. Fred. He told my mother that he had a concussion. Dr. Fred also told my mother that he would give Jim an excuse to stay out of school for the last three weeks, and he would take him home with him and teach him himself, which he did. He taught him the metric system, fractions, and decimals. He also was allowed to read some anatomy books. I missed walking to and from school with him. He was home after school and weekends. Jim was an asset when we played imaginary games.

When I was in fourth grade, we were studying Abraham Lincoln one morning. I drew a log cabin, but it looked so stupid, I took it home and showed it to my mother. I said, "It doesn't look right." Mother replied, "Do you want me to show you how to do it right?" She showed me how to do it in perspective. I went back to school after lunch and showed the kids how to do it. The teacher came in and the class began. She asked us to pass in our pictures. Then she held mine up in front of the class and said, "Who did this?" I proudly said, "I did!" She tore it up and put it in the waste basket. She said, "If I want your mother to draw a picture I will ask her." I said, "Mother didn't do it, I did!" All the kid said, "Mary Lee did it! We saw her do it, and she showed us how!" The teacher just turned and walked away. When I got home my mother said, "Well, if she wants you to do it the dumb way, do it the dumb way. It doesn't matter, the point is you know how to do it right."

I loved to play the games at school, at recess. Dodge ball is not played now here, because you would get hurt when the ball was thrown to get you out. One team was in the middle of the circle, while the other team threw the ball to put them out. We ran relays, and played blind man's bluff, balanced on a beam, and jumped rope.

Playing marbles was my favorite game because boys and girls could play together. The city schools had a contest, and I was chosen to represent my school. The contest was to take place on a Saturday morning. Friday afternoon, after school, two boys challenged me to play with them. I won all their marbles with my "agee" shooter. They were furious! One boy, Harold English, grabbed all my marbles in my bag and ran with them. I chased him, knocked him down, breaking one of his front teeth. I cut my knuckle on his tooth. I still have the scar. I took my marbles and went home. His mother called my father who took me to Harold's home with my marbles. Harold hid behind his mother's skirt and stuck out his tongue at me. I told him I was sorry I broke his tooth, period. My father threw my marbles in the lake, and forbade me to ever play again. My father said that my temper caused the boy permanent injury, and I must never fight again, except in self-defense. And I never did. Lesson learned.

Norman Rockwell painted a picture of this contest with the two boys that shows this perfectly. I have it. The blond boy even looks like Harold! How did he know?

I was in several plays in school. One Christmas, I was Bob Crochet's mother. When the scene opened, we began to speak our parts. The audience laughed! We forgot our parts and the teacher closed the curtain. Bob Crochet's head came to my shoulder, and Tiny Tim was taller than all of us. Poor casting! After the laughing stopped, the teacher raised the curtain again, we remembered our parts and the play continued. Mrs. Moats, Edgar and Jim, came to see the play. Another time I was the spirit of Maryland in a pageant. I was very dignified walking up the steps to the stage, I turned around slowly, raised my hands – and sneezed! Once again, the audience laughed. My parents never came to school events.

I was a school boy patrolman in fourth grade, one of two lieutenants in fifth grade, and the captain in the sixth grade. Our duties were to be crossing guards at the street corners around the school. When I was captain, there was a national convention of school patrolboys in Washington, DC. President Roosevelt was to be there to review our parade, but he threw the opening ball at a baseball game instead! We were disappointed but were still thrilled to march down Pennsylvania Avenue with so many other children. After the parade we got to go to the zoo. It was my first time. Unfortunately, I wore new shoes that made my feet bleed so I put them around my neck.

The Neighborhood Gang

Here are some of our experiences as part of what we called "our gang." The leader was a young teen, Harry Boyd. He was the son of the Irish family that lived in a basement apartment of a house down the street. When we were under his leadership, we never got into trouble. When Mike Cashman, another young teen who went by "Bubba", led us, we faced many dangers. I was next in age, and the only girl. In order to be part of the gang, I dressed in boys clothes (Harry's), put my hair under his cap, and was called Peter. My brother was next, and then Jackie Sergeant, who was about Jim's age. Neil Baylor was the youngest. Neil was a "mama's boy". If she was not home when he got home from school, he sat on the porch and cried loudly. He did the same thing when he got lost, until we found him. Many years later, my mother told me that he was in Italy during WWII. He got lost from his platoon, and just sat down until the enemy captured him.

Some Saturday mornings, we went to the museum in the park, where we could sit on the floor and copy any picture we wanted. They provided paper, pens, crayons, and pencils. We all loved to do this. Saturday afternoon, we usually went to the movies. The fare was twenty-five cents. There were two movie theaters across the street from one another. Each had a cowboy or other popular children's movie followed by a serial. A "punch–out ticket" was given at the beginning of the serial. If all tickets were punched at the end of the serial, the next movie and the first serial was given free. We were watching the serial, "The Last of the Mohicans". We did not like that the Indians were obviously white men.

One Saturday, the cowboy movie ended abruptly when the cowboy's horse stumbled and fell. The screen went black. The manager came out and explained that the cowboy had died. We filed out, and gathered at the corner and discussed what to do. We decided to go back, and each asked for ten cents back. The manager said, "No". The manager of the other theater crossed the street and offered to give us free tickets to his cowboy movie, and his serial story, "Rin-Tin-Tin", about the adventures of a German shepherd. We never went back to the other theater.

Whenever I see fliers for a circus coming to town, I think of one exciting adventure I had with the gang when I was eleven years old. Jim and I were "the lookouts" for the circus train because we could see it on the railroad tracks on top of the hill beyond the swamp in back of our house.

Finally, at 6AM one hot morning in July, we saw the Barnum and Bailey circus train on the tracks. We told our mother and raced down the street to alert the gang and get a boys outfit for me from Harry Boyd's mother. The circus would not let girls help to set up the circus. My disguise included boy's shoes and a cap to hide my hair. I also became "Peter". We gulped some juice and cocoa, some biscuits and a hot dog, and were off!

We got to the field in time to see the elephants pulling ropes to set the "Big Top" up. They use tractors now. The smaller tents were already up. We reported to a man in front of a tent where there were about twenty other boys. He assigned my brother and me to a worker who showed us how to water the animals. It was hard work and took much of the morning. We got buckets from a well at the edge of the field. The animals in the cages had places to empty the buckets outside of the cage which emptied into the cage. There were places for food, too, which we used later. The horses, mules, and camels drank from the buckets. The camels were mean and spit in our faces sometimes. Later we watered the elephants and one squirted me all over with water. Was I mad! Then everyone laughed at me, and I did, too!

As we worked, we got to see the performers before and after they got ready to perform in the parade. What a transformation! The women wore a lot of makeup, which was strange to us then, and had large muscles we saw before they covered them up with fabulous clothes. The men had some make up, too, but their muscles we expected to be big. We had never heard such a loud band, either and they sounded awful when they were tuning up, but wonderful when they got it right. We all were fed fried chicken, corn on the cob, biscuits and I had Coca-Cola to drink for the first time.

A clown called me over to his tent after we ate. When he turned around, inside the tent he said "Take off your cap." When I did, he put one of his stocking caps that he used to cover his head when he was in costume, on my head and tucked my hair under it. Then he said, "Run along, sonny." I asked, "Are you going to turn me in?" But he shook his head and laughed. He later let me watch him put his makeup on before the parade – what a lot of work it was to get the red nose just right and the eyebrows and especially the big mouth!

We got to see the "freaks", too. A very thin, tall man, a very huge lady, a man with one eye in his forehead a very ugly woman and man and several dwarfs. We heard them talking to each other, laughing and joking. As we said later "They are real people like other grownups!"

When the parade was over, we got to see the circus performance free. What a thrill that was to see the wonderful way the people and animals performed! We felt we knew them!

Afterwards we tried to sneak under the tent to see the Wild West Show because that was not free for us, but the bouncers picked us up and put us to work cleaning up the trash and watering and feeding animals as they got ready to leave. We worked until suppertime, then got candy, cotton candy and Coca-Cola before heading for home.

We were still excited and happy, knowing we would relive and remember this day as long as we lived!

The next stories will be about some adventures that we had on weekends, or during the summers, which deepened our faith and trust in God to look after us.

We decided to revisit the limestone quarry in the back of the railroads, on the hill, behind our house, where we had played many Saturday mornings in the summer. There was a high fence with warning signs "DANGER – BLASTING" and "NO TRESPASSING," of course, which we ignored because we knew they never blasted on Saturdays or Sundays.

After climbing over the fence, we climbed the rocks to a cave we could see from the bottom of the quarry. There we played pirates, after exploring the very interesting cave. We had read Treasure Island and pretended we were the characters. Suddenly, Harry yelled, "I see someone on top of the quarry!" We all ran to the opening, and sure enough, there was a group of men standing there, looking at us and yelling, "Don't move!" We froze. In a few minutes two men climbed down to us and helped us to the top, across from where we had been. They held on to us as a man pushed down on a black bar and the whole side of the quarry where we had been, crashed with a roar and dust into the bottom of the quarry!

After a stern lecture while we watched a railroad car being loaded with the limestone from trucks, the men took us down to the engine and helped us climb into the engine. We rode to the main office. What a thrill! We watched the engineer open the furnace and shovel in coal and saw him blow the whistle as we approached a road. The noise, heat and steam was awesome!

At the office, our parents were called and we all got strapped, but it was worth it! On Monday, we were heroes at school, too! We never went to the quarry again, especially as we thought about what the owner said – the limestone was going to a blast furnace and all trace of us would have disappeared forever.

I made balsa wood airplanes for the boys, usually models that didn't fly from pictures they gave me and wood we got from the Martin Airplane Factory (probably not the correct name – they made bombers during WWII, my dad said.) On this day, they wanted a larger plane that had a propeller and could fly. Bubba had a drawing that I could go by. They wanted to get the wood from the factory on a Saturday when they threw away lots of wood and also sold some thing we might use – bamboo strips and pieces of metal. I had some money in my piggy bank, but the boys were in a hurry, so I took some money from my mother's purse.

After climbing the fence, we walked across the field toward the plant. My heel was bleeding from my new shoes, so I asked the boys to lift me up on the wing of a plane that as sitting in the sun. I climbed down and put my head on the seat of an open cockpit. There was a space for a parachute in front of the seat, the pilot's cockpit was in front of mine. I took off my shoe and settled down to wait for the boys. Soon I fell asleep.

Suddenly, the plane reared and shook – we were moving! I tried to get up, but couldn't at first. We were airborne and circling! I struggled to my knees on the seat and the sash of my dress was untied and sailed past the pilot into the propeller! The pilot raised up and saw me, turned around and made a quick landing. He then helped me out of the plane, placed me on his lap on the ground and proceeded to spank me and cry, "I could have killed you! I was going to test the plane with a loop!" I had never seen a grown man cry, and in spite of my own pain, I felt sorry for him.

Of course, I got a strapping too, but I was convinced that God saved me and was punishing me for stealing my mother's money – I repaid her and never stole again. Yes, I made the plane and it flew beautifully, but the boys wouldn't let me fly it and they eventually wrecked it. I refused to make another one. Years later, I saw an airplane, just like the one I was in, suspended from the ceiling, at O'Hare Airport in Chicago.

One Saturday the gang decided to go swimming in a limestone quarry on the other side of the river. To reach it, we had to cross a long trestle, the longest one in Maryland, the boys said. It was wooden and had wooden platforms along the side at regular intervals with wooden barrels filled with water. The trestle started on a hill, and curved to cross the river. At first, we could easily step from one plank to another, but as we rounded the curve, the intervals were farther apart and we held hands to help each other. Suddenly, when we were about half way across the valley, we heard a train whistle blow!

Startled, we headed for a barrel platform – it was too small to hold all six of us! As fast as we could on hands and knees, Jim, Neil, and I crawled to the next platform – just in time! Around the bend came the train, whistle blowing, steam pouring out, men shaking their fists and yelling "God save you!" The trestle was swaying and groaning long after the train had passed. We were afraid to move at first, but finally decided we had better keep going across, since it was shorter than going back. However our adventure was not over. When we reached the other side, there was a rattler in the path! The oldest boy, Mike, took a long stick and flipped it into the bushes.

The quarry was within sight, so the boys ran and jumped in, only to find out that the sides were sheer and there was no way out! I ran to a farmer about a half mile away. He brought his tractor and ropes and pulled the boys out. Needless to say, he called our parents to come take us home and we all were strapped with our father's belts – standard punishment in those days.

When I was in sixth grade, conditions at home were very bad.

My Grandpa Lee and Grandma came to stay briefly because his business partner had taken the money from the business and committed suicide, leaving his wife and two children. Grandpa had sold the business and much of his possessions to provide for them and his employees. He found jobs for many including Jimmy McWiggan, his foreman who helped him later in Niagara Falls.

At first, Grandma was well and she wanted me to play with the little girls of a lady she had met who lived several blocks away, instead of the boys. She took me to a tea party at their house. The adults were in the house and we were on the patio. When we finished our tea and cookies, I taught them how to make mud pies, skin the cat on a tree branch, and walk the fence. We were really having fun when one of the girls fell off the fence and skinned her knee! Her cries brought the adults and the tea party ended with my disgrace. I was never invited back.

Grandma got sick and Grandpa was knocked down during a wild drinking party down stairs. They moved to Canada with a doctor he knew until he got a job with another roofing company and moved to Elizabethtown, PA selling roofing from farm to farm.

Jim and I had to fend for ourselves much of the time from then on.

At school, Mrs. Gutelius, the principal, was my sixth-grade teacher. She was a firm, but loving person. Her son was a policeman who came to our house at night when the parties got too loud. When that happened, we often went to Harry Boyd's apartment in the basement of the house where they were servants. They left the door open for us and allowed me to sleep with their little daughter "wee Jean" and Jim slept with Harry. In the morning they fed us oatmeal and tea, no questions asked.

One day, I was crying, alone, at recess after a particular hard night. Mrs. Gutelius came looking for me. She put her hand on my shoulder and said, "You can't help how your parent's act. My son was there last night. Pray for them! God gave you a good mind and a healthy body. He expects you to use them. I need a captain for my dodgeball team. Wash your face and hands and get outside to the playground!" I have never forgotten those words.

One Friday that spring, we were hungry. We hadn't eaten in a couple of days because there was no food in the house and our parents were gone. We didn't know where they were. Harry Boyd's family was on vacation. A friend of mine in sixth grade, Betty Weiner, said they were going to have a special dinner at their house that evening. I said to my brother "Why don't we go later after dinner, they might have left over's to give us, I think they will do that".

That night we knocked on the back door and a man with a funny little hat on his head came out. We told him we were hungry and asked for some left over's. He talked with someone in the house and came back out and said "No but you can come on in and share the meal with us." It was the Seder meal. We knew enough from Sunday school about the Seder and that it was a Jewish meal. The man spoke Yiddish but he explained everything in English as the meal went along. He said they always had an extra place at the table for the Messiah. I'll never forget that. Some of what we ate tasted terrible but after that we had a nice meal of lamb. God provided for us. My brother said "Well Jesus was a Jew so he would have taken us in too." Betty's father told us that we could come anytime we were hungry and they would feed us. We did this several times before school was out.

Our great grandpa Owings had died and left my father a lot of money. He sat and wrote checks giving the money away when he was drunk. One man he wrote checks to used the money to invest in a cement factory and made a fortune. Later, when I needed help for my father who was in a drunk tank in a Baltimore Police Station, I called that man because I knew dad had financed him. He threatened to put me in jail if I harassed him.

There was a lot of arguing at home. My father brought other women home. Mother left and had an apartment downtown. I went to visit and saw a hole in her apartment door. Mother said that Thelma, a friend of my father, had shot through the door. She showed me where the bullet had gone into the wall. She said that when she saw Thelma through the tiny peephole in the door she felt she had to move away, so she was not shot. She heard Thelma crying so she went to her and brought her into the apartment and asked her why she tried to shoot her. Thelma told her that my father told her mother would not give him a divorce. Mother showed her the divorce papers. She told her she would not tell on her. Mother showed me the gun, which she kept. She was Thelma's friend from then on and wrote to her until she died.

When I kissed Mother goodbye, I didn't know I would not see or hear from her for four years. My father married Thelma. When I got home, Dad told me to go upstairs and get some clothes, that he was taking us to visit Mrs. Sargent and her children. They had moved to Berkeley Springs, West Virginia. Jim took clothes and his teddy bear, and I took clothes and my Bible.

Berkeley Springs

Mrs. Sargeant had divorced her husband and moved with her three children. Jackie was the oldest and we had played with him in our gang. Virginia Lee was six now and Vandever was four. They had not been allowed to play with us. Their house was on the main street. We had electricity, but the rooms were heated with pot belly stoves filled with wood. There was a stove in the kitchen, too. It had a separate well which heated water. We had a bathroom with no tub. We took baths in a big round metal tub in the kitchen. That was used to do the wash, too.

A whole new way of life opened for me. I learned to cook and clean and help with the wash and the care of the other girls. There was time to play, too, and I was allowed to wear pants borrowed from a neighbor boy. Jim learned to do yard work and chop wood for the stoves and play with other boys in the neighborhood.

School was very different. I was in seventh grade. Families were very large, some 20 or more children. Some were needed to work at home, so they came to school in shifts and the teacher sent work home for them and asked them to come in when they needed to, in exchange for the regular students. There were no pencils and paper. We had four sided slates, instead. Books were shared with two or three others. The teacher wrote information on the board, gave us time to memorize it, then erased it!

On my first day the teacher said, "I will give you some problems. Write the answers on your slate." I was copying the problems on all four sides of my slate, when she said "Pass your slates in." I raised my hand and said "I just got them copied. I didn't have time to work them." She said, "Didn't you hear me say to put the answers on the slate?" "Yes, but I didn't have time to work them." "What do you mean? I didn't tell you to copy them. Work them on your abacus." I said, "What's an abacus?" The class laughed. The teacher said, "Stay after school." I had seen the children playing with beads strung above their desks. I learned to do the problems quickly.

There were practical math lessons, too. Farmers brought wagon loads of produce or cords of wood to the school. Lessons stopped and the teacher consulted with the farmer and inspected his load, then came into the class and presented the problem. "He has so much produce or cords of wood. One unit is so much. How much money should he charge when he sells it?" Community service!

We had a community spelling bee at school. All the words had to be from the Bible as that was the only book many people had in their homes, I was told. One elderly man had always won it, for many years, so they had a second prize to keep the competition going. The year we were there, a teenager from our school won it!

Many of the children came to school barefoot with their shoes around their necks. They washed their feet at the pump and put on their shoes for school. Wrestling was a favorite sport for the boys. We girls sat on the fence between the playgrounds to watch. A new man teacher came, so the boys challenged him to wrestle their champion. The teacher won, then told them he wasn't a city man as they had thought. He was from the hill country too!

I had my first experience with the death of a child there. A student in my class had an ear infection that killed him. We went to the funeral. He was one of twenty children in that family. A visitor said to her friend "Well, she has nineteen left." A relative turned to her and said, "Which of your children should God take?" So unkind!

There I first became interested in handicapped people. I had a friend named Patience who took me to visit her family in the hills. They had no electricity or running water and the wooden cabin had only three rooms. The kitchen was the living room, too. They had an outhouse, another new experience for me. She took me to tiny bedroom where her brother laid. He was a teenager she said. His arms and legs were contracted. His hands and fingers could move as he communicated with them. He could not talk. She changed and cleaned him and then we carried him outside and placed him in a special chair they had made for him. He enjoyed watching the trees and the birds. She taught me to communicate with him and told him stories. He seemed to understand and laughed when it was funny. He could shake his head for yes and no. She would tell him something funny and he would laugh. He knew what she was talking about. If she made a mistake when telling him a story, he would shake his head as if to say, opium

"No, that wasn't right." He seemed intelligent and loved by his family. They told me that God made him that way for them to take care of him and love him. I never forgot that. Patience came to visit me in Janesville many years later.

I had a second experience with a handicapped person here, too. A young man with Down's syndrome used to come to the indoor swimming pool we played in often that summer. He sat on the edge of the pool with his feet in the water when there were a number of us playing and ducking each other. One day when the adult assigned to supervise us was busy elsewhere, I dove off the deep end and swam underwater to the shallow end of the pool. He put his foot on my back. I swam faster. He moved with me until his entire weight was on my back. My knees and elbows scraped the bottom of the pool as I fought to come up! I lost consciousness.

The adult had come back, seen the situation, ordered him off me, and someone pulled me out of the water. She got me to breathe again. I still have scars on my knees. I cannot swim under water now because I feel his weight. He was forbidden to come into the pool room at first. He cried on a bench outside until I went to the supervisor and asked if he could be there when a grownup could be with him and she agreed. We kids even gave him a birthday party because we knew he didn't want to hurt me.

Mrs. Sargeant was Catholic so we went to her church. I was puzzled because I did not understand what the priest was saying. The liturgy was in Latin then, except for the sermon, but I didn't stay that long. I left each Sunday and went to a protestant church in the next block. Jim stayed with the family. I was scolded each Sunday for doing this.

There was a castle that we wanted to see on a mountain nearby, so Jim and some boys decided to go by the road to see it. I decided it would be faster and more fun to climb up to it through the woods. I had to go around a ledge because I had no hand hold to pull myself up with. When I looked down on the ledge, it was full of rattlesnakes sunning themselves! I would have been bitten for sure! The castle was very interesting. Modeled after one in Europe, they said. It was so damp and cold. I wouldn't want to live there.

We had been with Mrs. Sargeant since July. My father stopped paying her. She told us that she was going to send us back to him for Christmas. She took us to Hancock, Maryland to a hotel lobby that was used as a bus station and bought tickets for us. The bus was to come that afternoon. It had started to snow hard. The bus did not come for three days because of the storm. We had water from the drinking fountain in the lobby, but no food. We pulled up the leather cushions and found some gum wrappers to chew for the sugar.

When we finally got on the bus, a lady on the aisle in front of us, opened a bag and began to eat some fried chicken. The odor made our stomachs growl. Finally, she let her hand fall down with a piece of chicken in it. My brother dove off his seat, grabbed it and stuck it in his mouth! She yelled! The bus stopped and the driver came back and told Jim that he would put both of us off the bus in the snow if he heard one sound from him. We were terrified and cried as quietly as we could.

When we got to Hagerstown we went to our house, but there was a strange woman living there who told us she didn't know where our father was. We decided to go to the hotel where the black man who had taken care of us worked. We sat outside, under the entrance roof to wait till he came out. We were cold, as we had only sweaters to wear when we left home. Our shoes were too small, so we had cut the toes off and wrapped them with tape.

A policeman came along and recognized me because I had been a school patrolman. He said that he didn't know where our father was, but our mother had gone to Europe with Jerry Harp, her friend who was a band leader. He made arrangements for us to go into the hotel to get warm until he got off duty in an hour. A lady there wrapped us up in a blanket. He came and took us to his house. It was about nine o'clock at night then. His wife fed us, but we ate too fast and vomited. He called Dr. Fred who said to feed us chicken soup and put us to bed when he heard our story.

The next day was Christmas! We had clothes under the tree. Hats, gloves, sweaters, shoes, boots and outfits! Evidently he had gone somewhere and taken up a collection. We took some clothes that were too small to Mrs. Sargeant's children too! Jim said, "We don't have anything to give you. If you will make a list and how much they cost, when I grow up, I'll pay you back" They laughed. He said, "It's not funny. You can't have things without paying for them." They explained they were a gift, but he said "Oh well. That's a good deal then." They decided to send us back to Mrs. Sargeant because we did not know where any relatives were and that was where my father left us. They took up another collection for the bus fare and called her. She met us at the hotel. She was upset to find out that no one knew where my father was, but she was kind to us.

We decided that God wanted us to stay with her and told her so. She agreed.

That spring, I had an experience that was frightening and painful, but God allowed it to happen so that I would understand and be able to help other people who had similar experiences.

Jim was late coming home from visiting with some friends in the hills, so I went looking for him. I met a strange man, who told me Jim was in an abandoned cabin around the next bend. When we got inside, he started kissing me, cutting my mouth. When I struggled and yelled, he choked me, raped me, broke my arm, then choked me again until I was unconscious. Then, thinking I was dead (as he later testified) he covered me with a tarp and went to get a shovel to bury me.

While he was gone, I recovered consciousness. I realized I wasn't dead because I was bleeding and hurting. I dragged myself from under the tarp, got my footing because I was dizzy, and went home as fast as I could. Mrs. Sargeant called the doctor who came right away, as his office was closed. He sat across the kitchen table from me as I sat on Mrs, Sargeant's lap. After washing the blood off and pouring iodine on the bone sticking out of my arm, he grabbed my hand and pulled hard until the end of the bone disappeared into the arm. He asked me to move my fingers. I could. He felt my arm to see if it was straight. It was. Then he sent Jim for a board and used Mrs. Sargeant's torn slip as a sling. I never got an infection and my arm works perfectly. Oh, Yes. We all prayed before he started working on me. My mouth healed without treatment except iodine. The sheriff was called.

Someone threw a stone through the window, so the sheriff decided to put me in jail for protection until the trial. They had arrested the man. I was in a cell opposite from him. There were rumors of a lynching, so more police were there. I stayed until the circuit judge came. I don't know how long. The man cried a lot and paced the floor. I had books to read and people came to talk to me. The priest came and explained what he was saying in the liturgy, and that he spoke English in his sermons. I told him I wasn't naughty, so why was I in jail and he told me to keep me safe. Then he told me that most of the disciples were in jail, too, and so was Jesus. He said we would not have the Bible we have if the disciples had not been in jail so they could write letters that are the epistles. He said that God wanted me to learn more about Him and he was sent to teach me. He came every day, and talked to the man too and prayed with us. He gave me an old crucifix and taught me the rosary.

I took the rosary to court when I testified and squeezed it so hard my hand bled. The judge sent me out to wash my hand, and when I came back the court was not in session again yet. I asked him if they were going to put a rope around the man's neck and kill him. He banged his gavel and told me no, that he would be fed and cared for but could never hurt little girls again. The man looked up, he had been crying, and seemed so relieved. I was glad for him. I learned to forgive him.

My Uncle Bob, who I did not know, was driving through Hancock, MD, when his car broke down. He bought a newspaper to work the crossword puzzle while he waited to get his car fixed. He saw the story and my name in the Hancock newspaper. He knew we had been missing from the family, so he called my Grandpa and Grandma Lee, who were living with him. They urged him to go down and bring us to them if he could. He came down and got directions to the priest, who called my grandparents and then went with Uncle Bob to Mrs. Sargeant's. Uncle Bob gave her twenty-five dollars for each of us. That was a lot of money those days. All he had to spare. He took us to Paxtang, Pennsylvania to be united to our family at last.

Paxtang

We were very happy to see Grandpa and Grandma Lee again. We had seen them last when they came to live with us in Hagerstown and wondered what had happened to them. We hadn't seen Aunt Jinny since she left York to be married. She had divorced that husband and married Uncle Bob since then. They had no children yet.

School was as I remembered in Hagerstown. There was a problem with the patrol boys there. They had been stopping busy traffic with long poles for longer than they should and there had been many complaints to the principal. When he found out that I had been a captain in sixth grade, he asked me about having girls as patrolmen. I told him that we had both boys and girls and that I had seen many girls in the parade in Washington. He decided to have all girls, since the boys had refused to behave all year. They weren't happy, but we did a good job and he was pleased.

It was very cold in January and February, so that the ice on the river in Harrisburg was very thick. When the thaw came, the ice broke up with thundering noise and actually cut the bank and some houses as it moved down stream. The dam broke upriver, resulting in a severe flood. The principal called my uncle and asked him if I could go to the riverside in Harrisberg with the patrol-girls to help the men working on the bridge. He agreed and we spent two days while school was closed running errands and taking food to the men on the bridge. Houses, barns, animals, and people were coming down the river on rooftops. They hit the bridge and they were crushed and sucked under the bridge. A crew of men threw lassoes and ropes to rescue the people. When they were pulled up the arch on the bridge broke their legs often, so ambulances were at the bridge, too. An old woman was yelling at the men, insisting that they rescue animals, too. One of the men begged me to get her to leave. I told her that the Masonic Lodge on the hill was looking for help with lost and injured children as some of our patrol had gone there. She ran off and the man hugged me!

I got to see my first baby there. A boat had gone to the rescue of a pregnant woman whose house was filled with water, but they couldn't get her through the second story window because she was too large and was in the last stages of delivery, so they climbed in and delivered her on a floating bed. They wrapped her in a sheet with the baby and put them in the rowboat. They called me to wade out and take the baby while they helped the woman to shore. I had never seen any baby before and this one had the placenta on its tummy – it was still attached. The baby was crying hard as I tried to comfort him. I went with them to the ambulance and rode to the hospital, where nurses took over. I went back to the bridge with many questions which grandma answered that night. Years later, on a trip back east, I needed directions to a home I had lived in in Elizabethtown, Pennsylvania. I asked a man who was walking his dog on the sidewalk. He was the man I helped on the bridge!

The flood was the first time I had experienced God's awesome power! The terrible destruction of buildings, animals and people. I saw the fear, anxiety, sorrow, pain, and hopelessness expressed by people, but also the joy and relief when they were rescued or found a loved one in the midst of pain and destruction. Then came the miracle of a new life! I was thankful to be a small part of the rescue team.

I had an adventure in a play there. We were dancing very fast. My partner let go of my hand and I fell off the stage, landing on a drum in the orchestra pit. Needless to say, that caused the play to stop. The drum was ruined and I had a big bruise. The play eventually resumed without further trouble.

One day, when we were walking home from school, our father drove up. He told Jim to get in the car. I objected and he told me that he would just take Jim, so I got in too. He took us to Brookeville, Maryland where my Uncle Laurie and Aunt Verdie lived.

Brookeville

Dad did not tell Aunt Jinny and Uncle Bob when he picked us up, so Aunt Verdie made him call them. She got some clothes for us and we settled down with their family.

The first thing I noticed was that there was a lot of salt and pepper on the food! I was not allowed to sleep by Jim and this was the first time we'd slept in separate rooms. He sneaked into bed with me several times before Aunt Verdie scolded him and Uncle Laurie talked to him. That began our separation that lasted until we moved to Niagara Falls. It was good for him to learn to be more on his own and to have boy friends, but we missed each other and were apart for much of the day as we had different chores.

Brookeville was a small village with homes on each side of one road. It was located on a hill with a grocery store and gas station combined at the top of the hill. Our house was two houses from the store, which was also the post office. The house at the bottom of the hill, on a curve, was the temporary capital of the United States for a brief time during the war of 1812 after the fire in Washington. At least, the plaque on the lawn in front of the house said so. There was a little village at the bottom of the hill where the black families who worked in our village lived. Aunt Verdie's house was two stories with a basement. Beside Aunt Verdie and Uncle Laurie, their two sons, John Beverly and Francis (Pete) lived with us. There were six bedrooms and an enclosed porch upstairs where Francis kept his traps and hung the pelts of animals he trapped. There was a small garden for vegetables and a chicken house in the back yard.

John Beverly worked at the Library of Congress in Washington and was writing a genealogy of the Riggs family which was published while we lived there. Aunt Verdie and I proofread it one summer. Francis was going to high school and graduated while we were there, I think. We became good friends and he took me to movies and plays. An older son had died of tuberculosis. Their oldest child, Eleanor Muncaster, was married to John and lived on a farm near there. I visited her often and worked on the farm with her.

I remember visiting the neighbors in the village. The woman who lived across the street invited us over and offered us candy. She had already taken a tiny bite out of each piece to see what was in it. Aunt Verdie said not to mention it as that was her habit. I visited the Howards, who lived in the former temporary capital, and remember an old organ that had pedals to push to make music.

I was learning to play with dice for stones on the back porch with Bob Dodson, a black man who cleaned our chicken house, when Aunt Verdie came home from church one Saturday afternoon. She had been practicing playing the organ for church. She sent me to my room immediately and scolded Bob. Then she came upstairs and told me that Bob had a gambling problem, that his family probably would not have food to eat if he gambled his money away, and that I was a bad influence on him. She said I must be a good example because I was white and he was black and couldn't help being weaker. She ordered me to cook a meal for his family and deliver it to their cabin, which was about a mile away. They were already eating when I arrived and wanted me to take the meal back to Aunt Verdie; I knew better than to do that!

Later, Bob was accused of murdering a white man who sold bootleg whisky to black people at his home near the village. Bob came to the house and told Uncle Laurie and he held Bob and cried. The only evidence against him was that a doctor had found him lying beside the road. The dying man's last words were, "Tell Bob..."

Everyone was sure he didn't do it and Uncle Laurie took me with him one day when he talked to Ol Macgruder to try to get him to testify for Bob. He asked if Uncle Laurie could promise he wouldn't have to work on the chain gang that summer. Uncle Laurie said he would have to be very careful not to get mixed up when he testified, or that might happen. He also told Uncle Laurie that the man had been drunk. He had fallen on the iron foot of his stove and hit his head. He said that Bob had left before the fall. Ol Macgruder had been drunk that night and had been singing "Old Man River" as he walked by our house. He had a beautiful voice. The moon was full and it was a warm night, so everyone knew he had been there that night. I know that Bob was given a "hung jury" that meant that he could be put in jail if he did anything else wrong Uncle Laurie said.

One night I heard someone downstairs, so I got up and walked down a few steps. I stopped because Uncle Laurie was standing in the hall with food smeared all over the front of him. Aunt Verdie was saying, "Laurie, you're going to get killed some time when you go out after the Klan!" He said, "If I can get them to stop once, it's worth it!" I went back to bed, but found out later what he was talking about. He would not take communion with men that were in the Klan. He took it from the pastor by himself. Our family went to a Protestant Episcopal church every Sunday in another town.

When the weather prevented people from going to church, the families in the village took in black families for worship. Aunt Verdie played the piano in the back hall for everyone and I heard songs I had never heard before, even in the black churches I had gone to with our maids in Hagerstown.

Our wash was picked up by two black girls every Saturday and returned on Monday. One Saturday, I heard talking downstairs when I was making beds with Aunt Verdie. I found the two girls sitting in our living room and told Aunt Verdie. She was angry and confronted them. They jumped up when they saw her. "I have something to tell you. No white person comes into my house unless I invite them. No white person sits in my living room unless I invite them to. You may not take the wash today. You must go home and get your father." They tried to object, but she insisted. When he came, he apologized and said that they were learning bad things in school. She told him that they could be accused of stealing and she didn't want them to get in trouble because she cared about them. He thanked her and said they ought to know better. I suggested that she get a washing machine and she was furious. She said, "Of course I won't ever get a machine!"

I learned to care about other people, even grown-ups and especially black people who did not have opportunity to earn much money. That it was what Jesus wanted me to do. There was prejudice, though, as if they weren't as smart as whites were. John Beverly came home from work one night and said that two black girls were sitting behind him on the bus and one said to the other, "Is you did your Greek yet?" Everyone at the table laughed and Aunt Verdie said, "They probably have white blood if they are going to college." I asked how they got white blood and she changed the subject.

Brookeville Society

We went to school in Sandy Springs on a bus – my first and last school bus experience. My Aunt Verdie had given me a list of last names of children I could associate with. I found out that they were the "in" group and I was accepted immediately – how nice! But I soon found out that they weren't nice to many of the other children, especially the poor or handicapped.

A crisis came when a girl with epilepsy had a seizure when bringing a full tray of hot soup from the kitchen one noon. She convulsed and the soup poured down her sweater. When she fell to the floor, the children laughed and so did the teacher! I ran to her and tried to pull the sweater from her body. She did not cry out, as she was still convulsing. I yelled at the teacher "Help her!" When she did not respond, I yelled "You are not fit to teach!" and ran to the office. No one was there, so I went to the file and called her adoptive mother on the phone. She said she would come immediately. Then I went back to the room and helped the child to the bathroom. When we took the sweater off, she was already beginning to blister!

I was expelled from school for three days. Aunt Verdie went to school with me and told the principal that I would need to get all my homework. She said she agreed with me that the teacher was at fault, but that I should not have been disrespectful. The injured girl was named Rosemary. Out of gratitude, her mother took us to the National Symphony series in Washington and many historic sites with several other poor girls. Rosemary later had poems published, married, and came to see me in Janesville before she died. As a result of my friendship with her, I was ostracized by the "in" group, but I didn't care.

I was in two plays there. I played the first witch in "Macbeth" and was supposed to throw the entrails into the charmed pot. I received a burned hand when I reached into a jar with chicken entrails soaked in formaldehyde! The Biology teacher was furious with the English teacher for taking that jar for the play. In another play, I wore a hoop skirt that I had received from Aunt Julia, an elderly relative who had a houseful of antiques. I sat down without folding the hoop because no one had instructed me. Of course, the skirt went over my head! The curtain was closed until I could recover. Fortunately, I had pantaloons on. The audience enjoyed it but I didn't!

My Latin teacher said we would never use Latin, so he read the paper to us. He made assignments and corrected them and gave us tests, but we never had to read aloud.

My father had gone to that high school and there was a plaque with his name and Sarah Chitchester as honor students on it.

I had two "coming out" parities when I was sixteen. The first one was at the home of Uncle Laurie's sister, Aunt Nan. She lived alone in the family mansion with an elderly black couple as servants. I wore my Sunday dress. All the guests were very elderly single men who were dropped off by relatives. We had punch that had alcohol in it and the combination of cake, ice cream and punch made the guests very drowsy. The black man played three tunes on the out of tune piano for us to dance to. Each man danced with me once after toasting me for the occasion. Then they settled down to sleep or talk politics with each other or Aunt Nan. At 10 PM the cars arrived to take us all home. Aunt Verdie's family really enjoyed my account of the party!

The second "official" introduction into society was in Howard County. The family's ancestral home was in Howard County, but the party was at some other location. I had to have two escorts who had correct bloodlines. Two of my cousins were chosen: Francis and young Harwood. My Aunt Dorothy made the dress. Because she was Quaker, it was grey, but had a satin sash. It covered me from my neck to the floor and had long sleeves, but it fit well and was pretty. When we left the house, she told the escorts to check my girdle, meaning my sash, but we all enjoyed a good laugh!

At the dance, I met a line of elderly gentlemen. Each man signed his name on a card on my wrist. Then I entered the ballroom where the young people were. Only waltzes were played and I always walked forward, the partners walked backward. They told me it was because of the trains women once wore. How silly! I danced once with each elderly man, then my escorts and then as other men asked me. I had fun and danced every dance!

I saw a beautiful redheaded girl at the dance and asked who she was. "Ask your Aunt Verdie," and funny looks was the only answer I received. I did ask her when I got home and she told me the story. During the "war between the States" as the civil war is called in the south, my great grandfather and his brother owned a plantation with slaves together in Howard County, Maryland, where my father was born. His brother helped slaves who were mistreated escape using an underground railroad. Great Grandfather found out about it and there was a duel in the barn. My great grandfather shot his brother. He then sold half of the estate and moved his brother's family to Baltimore County with all his possessions and the money. The redhead was from that side of the family. She told me there was now a small village with the Owings name where many black people lived.

One summer Aunt Ada invited me to the eastern shore where they had a cottage. She told Aunt Verdie that I could go swimming, horseback riding and social events with my cousin Genevieve who was my age. Uncle Laurie didn't believe that was why I was invited. He said she just wanted a free babysitter for the two younger children. I said that was ok with me, if I could have fun, too, so I went. Uncle Laurie was right. He came down two weeks later and sat with the little ones while I went swimming for the first time. I did get to go to a dance the night before he came. My cousin Dick came, got a babysitter, ordered me to put on a dress of Genevieve's, and took me to the dance where his sister and mother were. They were furious! Then he called Uncle Laurie to come and get me. He and Aunt Ada had words before we left and he told Verdie, "I told you so!"

While we lived with Aunt Verdie in Brookeville, my father visited. He sometimes took me to Washington, DC, where he drove a taxi. His wife, Thelma, was in Puerto Rico, working for the government, I think.

I only remember one time that I bought a new dress. My father took me from Brookville to Washington, DC, to go shopping. The dress was navy blue with a big navy blue satin sash and a little bolero with plastic red cherries. He bought me stockings, shoes and a brooch. I remember how upset my aunt was with him spending all that money on me. She wanted him to take everything back to the store. He refused. There was no joy in wearing those new clothes because my wearing them upset my Aunt Verdie. I didn't wear the dress at all until I went to Niagara Falls.

My father was a typical alcoholic. After his shift ended at midnight, he would go from tavern to tavern meeting friends and drinking. I was always greeted warmly and given ginger ale and pretzels. He was greeted with "Hi, Stanley, is this your little girl?

She's growing up. How old are you, honey?" I came to appreciate how much he needed to relate to these people. He was very lonely. The only way I could get him to take me home was to tell him that I wanted to stay up later. Then he played the concerned Dad and insisted I go home to bed.

One night, a man came up to him in the tavern and whispered something to him. He acted very worried and told me to go to the cab and wait. In a few minutes, he came out and drove to a different neighborhood. He told me I must never tell anyone what was going to happen. He took me down some steps to a basement door that had a peephole in the door. They let us in.

It was a bare room with a couple of tables and chairs, a bar on one side and a curtained doorway in the back. My father told me to sit at a table and be quiet. There was only the big black bartender and myself. Then my father went behind the curtain. There was a sweet, smell, like perfume in the place. After a little while, a black child came pounding on the door. "The cops are coming!" he yelled. The bartender grabbed me, took dirty towels out of a big wastebasket, lifted me in, and said "Shut up, kid, and be still!" I heard people moving, banging, shouting, then the door shutting and more banging. Quiet. I crawled out to a dark room. The door had been nailed shut. I cried myself to sleep.

The next morning, I saw a window above the sink on the alley. It had bars on the outside. I couldn't get the window open, so I broke it with a chair. Then I worked on the rusted bars to get out. An old man was lying in the alley with a bottle. Between us, we got the bars loose and he pulled me out. When he found out where my Dad lived, he said he'd take me there. We started to walk down the alley together, but he turned to me and said, "If a cop saw me walking with a girl, he would arrest me, sure. Get behind me and follow a little ways behind." So I did.

When we got to the apartment, it was locked, so I sat on the steps and cried. It was Sunday morning and the lady across the hall came out dressed for church. When she saw me, she took me in her apartment and called my uncle who came and took me home. Uncle Larry told me not to tell Aunt Verdie. He took me to his daughter Eleanor to get cleaned up. He said I never would have to visit my Dad again, and I never did. He said the sweet smell was opium and that my Dad had been arrested. I was 14 at this time.

That was the second time God sent a homeless man to rescue me!

Jim and I visited Aunt Edith and Uncle Henry for a weekend one summer. They had no living children. They lived in a mansion on a farm. They were wealthy, with servants working in the house and hired manager in charge of running the farm. They did not know how to talk with us, but they taught us to play bridge, which we really enjoyed.

We also visited with Aunt Dorothy and Uncle Harwood and their children, Margaret and young Harwood, Jr. They lived on a farm across the road, but were not so wealthy. A farm family worked with them and their children. The first weekend we stayed with them, their hired man was killed and partially eaten by their sow. They said she was crazed by the smell of blood from a wound on his leg. Uncle Harwood raised the farmer's children as his own from then on.

Aunt Dorothy was a Quaker and wore a little white cap on her head all the time. She said the Bible said women must cover their heads when they pray, and she never knew when she might need to pray. We went to the Quaker meeting house with the family. There was no altar or cross or anything on the walls. Everyone read their Bibles and spoke about what they read when they wanted to. They asked for prayers for problems and gave thanks for answered prayers. There was an elder who began and ended the meeting with a prayer. Then we went to a potluck meal together.

We heard the banns announced, giving public notice that two Quakers intended to marry. The man passed the quiz by the men there, and was cleared to marry. The woman had not taken care of a baby under two, so she had to go to a lady who let her take care of her children. After spending time taking care of the children, she, too, passed and they could be married.

We saw the wedding, too. There were no special clothes. The man's family was on one side of the church and the woman's on the other side. There was a ribbon tied to each front pew. An elder listened to their vows, first to God, then to each other, then to the congregation, then they tied a knot in the ribbon and each one cut it from the front pew. I whispered, "That must be where the term 'tie the knot' came from!" They did not have rings as they don't believe in jewelry.

All three families, Uncles Laurie, Henry, and Harwood, went to different churches, but I saw all of them living Christian lives – showing love and concern for those around them regardless of color or status, reading the Bible, praying, going to church, and having fellowship with others.

One summer we also visited Grandpa and Grandma Lee who had moved to Elizabethtown, Pennsylvania. Grandpa had a new job selling roofing to Pennsylvania Dutch farmers. He took me with him several times as he went around to their farms. One time, a woman holding something in her apron came up to her husband while he was standing near the car window. She said, "It's a boy, Abel." She had had the baby while working in the field! He told her, "Go up to the house. You don't have to get supper."

Great Grandma Lee came to visit. I asked her why she and Grandma and Grandpa didn't go to church. She said that many years ago in Detroit, she had delivered a 15-year-old Irish girl who had been raped by her employer and had placed the girl and her baby with a Christian family. Her church had said she and her two teenaged sons could not come to church because she had caused her sons to associate with a person of ill repute. She said, "God gave power for men to say who can go to church, but no man can keep me out of heaven." She fell and broke her hip. She told us she would get pneumonia and die because she had a bad cold and was 91 years old. She showed us how to put traction on her leg with a large tomato can, and how to care for her until she died as she predicted.

Aunt Jinny and Uncle Bob had moved to Hershey, PA, and we experienced a real vacation when we went to visit them! We toured the chocolate factory, swam in the city pool, and played in the amusement park. We saw the famous Norwegian figure skater, Sonya Hening, fall on the ice during her show. They shut the performance down for an hour while the ice was prepared for her grand entrance. We saw a Broadway play, too. We ate at the Hershey Hotel and read that the governor had been arrested there for bringing whiskey into the hotel for a party, which was against the law in Hershey.

I had three experiences on John and Eleanor's farm that I remember. I was assigned by John's mother, Mrs. Aletta, to work in the field with the black men. Gus was in charge of the field workers and asked me if I had been naughty and was being punished with working in the field. I assured him I hadn't. He assigned me to gather the corn stalks instead of cutting them, since he objected to me working in the fields at all. We spent the morning thinning corn. At noon, he took me to the "big" house as the blacks called the main mansion. He asked Mrs. Aletta to put me to work in her house instead of the field. He said I burned and he didn't, and that it wasn't proper for a white girl to ever work in the field. They were prejudiced, too!

One night in the spring, all the white and black men were very sick with the flu. Eleanor and I had to bring the ewes into the barn to have their lambs because we were the only able-bodied workers. It was pouring rain. We found all ewes in the field and many had

had their lambs already. Foolishly, we took all the ewes to the barn first and then brought the lambs. The ewes would not nurse any lamb but their own, but we had mixed them all up. Some lambs died in the process. When we told the men, they told us to skin the dead lambs, fasten it on a live lamb, and take it to a mother that we remembered where she had lain. While we saved a few that way, we had to hand feed the rest of the lambs all summer with the milk from the ewes who refused to let any lamb nurse directly!

Eleanor was on bed-rest upstairs about a week after having given birth to Edwin, her first child. I was faced with preparing the noon meal for eight men who were harvesting. I had two coal oil stoves – one in the house and one on the back porch. I had butchered chickens and placed them in buckets of hot water to get them ready to get their feathers off. I had a bushel of potatoes to peel, and corn to shuck, then boil. A young man named George Reuss arrived with a bushel of tomatoes to can. I tried to send him back to Mrs. Aletta, who had sent him. No luck! Eleanor called out the window to ask who the man was and I said, "He's a new worker and he looks like Andy Gump!" George went to the University of Virginia until Bill, John's younger brother, brought him home with him to work on the farm and earn some money.

I knew I couldn't get the meal and the tomatoes done in time. Sarah, the black lady who worked on the farm, hadn't come yet. Just then, I saw her walking down the road, but she only had her smallest children with her. She saw the mess I was in and sent the biggest child running for the older children. In no time we were ready for the men – just as they came from the field!

This story is an article I wrote about Sarah for a college paper.

Sarah's Story

Sarah was brown and round, warm and soft, clean and mended, strong and quick, happy and sad, and stern and loving. I first saw her striding down the dirt road in the early dawn, toward the farm house where I had been sent to work, with her smallest baby in one arm, the next in the other, and a third running to keep up. Her graying hair was neatly braided around her head, her apron flapped in the breeze that her purposeful walk made, a small cotton sack hung from her waist (containing her own tools, I later found out, knives razor sharp, honed by her special stone), her brown bare feet sent up little spurts of dust as she hurried. She was ready for canning season to begin; ready to do her share, and more, to provide food for two white families and her own, which numbered eighteen at that time.

I came to echo my cousin's exclamation, "Thank Heavens she's come, now I can face the day!" Each day steadily went by, the work diminishing with our energy until at the end, we could all look at each other and join her as she said wearily, yet with pleasure, "Well, Miss

Eleanor, it's done! Jest look at them cans!" And there they stood, shining on the shelves and stacked neatly in her box to take home, glowing in the lamplight. "Look at us! We're proud too!" This was Sarah. She had a firm pride in herself, her own family, and her two white families; The important one at the "big house," and the smaller, less important one, in our "little house."

She reminded me of my own curious place in her white world. "Remember, you're quality. You may have to work like a field hand, because of what your pappy done, but it won't hurt you none. You got the same blood they has. The thing is, you got to act it, and not uppity either. You do what Jesus wants and you'll turn out as good as any of them at the 'big house.'"

There was only one set of rules; she applied this philosophy to her own children too. "You ain't jest any no count field hand! Behave yo'self so's Jesus and Miss Alletta kin be proud of you!" I was "Miss Mary Lee" to her, but she slapped me when I was "sassy" or "uppity" and spanked me soundly when I insisted, at sixteen, that shorts were proper attire to wear around the negro men who worked on the farm. "You want them men to think you're no count white trash? You jest behave like quality folks or I'll learn you how!" When I complained to my aunt, I was quietly reminded, "Sarah has the same standards for her own girls.

They're decent Christian negroes. I agree with her." And that ended that.

Sarah's babies were part of her: The older two seemed to grow from her skirt and the tiniest seemed to be part of her breast or shoulder. I was amazed at how she could work at such a steady pace and yet never cease to care for them. Rarely was the baby put down in its box, but both her hands were free to peel and core the fruit even when she nursed him. The two older babies toddled outside to answer nature's calls on the ground occasionally, while she worked on, talking to them, singing to them, feeding them bits of fruit. When they were too tired to stand or sit, they curled up at her feet to sleep. One of her older children popped in occasionally to ask a question or to relay a message. The pattern of rapport between Sarah and her older children remains an ideal of mine. There was a warm bond of friendship based on mutual respect between them, cemented with a love that was almost tangible.

Sarah's simple faith was the source of her courage to face her many problems. With the conceit that only a thirteen year old can possess, I undertook to teach her the "proper" way to pray, on her knees, hands folded, eyes closed, by her bed, etc. Instead of wherever she happened to be, hands still for a few seconds (but remaining in working position), eyes open, head thrown back, talking to

Jesus. Her answer? "You believe Jesus is everywhere, even in this room?" Of course, I had to answer "Yes!"

Her response, "Then why can't I talk to Him?" Even I had no answer to that!

Practical common sense and rich earthy humor, tempered with love toward "all of God's children," that was Sarah: Yet more than anyone else, she taught me that black and white are two worlds. On the nights when "trouble was riding" she was tense and fearful, praying aloud while washing dishes, or singing mournful hymns, waiting for her man, Gus, the proud possessor of Five Gold Teeth, to walk her home. On those nights, she was evasive, and when pressed, exclaimed, "Don't bother me child, this is my own business and the business of us colored folks!" When I asked to go to church with her, as I had gone with a negro nursemaid as a child in another city, she said "You go to your own and let us go to someplace where we can be ourselves before God!" with so much feeling, I never mentioned it again.

A joy of life was part of her being. "Hello, there. Open your eyes and look at the purty world Jesus made you," she'd say to the new baby animals when they were still wet from birth. "Look at you, stickin' your little head outen' the ground already to look at the sun," she'd address the garden plants. But death was part of life too, and just as natural. "Well, Mr. Rooster, your time is up" as she carried him, squawking, to the chopping block. "Do it quick, ain't no call to make anything suffer. When your time comes, then maybe God'll take you quick an' easy too!" When her baby died, "Ain't no call to try to think like Jesus. Maybe He know'd it'd have a hard time down here. Lord, my arms feel empty though!"

Sarah possessed a "sixth sense" according to the white folks. She "had a spirit" according to the Negroes. She did not like this, yet felt "obliged" to tell what she felt was revealed to her. She was not sure that it was "right" and prayed that she would not be burdened with this gift anymore. She told me that I would marry a gangly eighteen year old, who had come to work for the harvest late one summer. I laughed heartily, since I had nicknamed him "Andy Gump" to the delight of all, both black and white. Besides, I had a "crush" on another boy at that time. Five years later, when I returned with him as my husband, she looked up from scrubbing the floor at the "big house," and said "I tole you so" and held out her arms for my baby.

She wanted us to take one of her older teenage girls up north with us to care for the baby, but when I explained that there were no negroes in the town and that I would not know how to supervise her finding a suitable husband, she replied "You're right, there's trouble here, but I guess it's everywhere, and I'd better be around to help them face it. At least here I know who's who!"

Sarah died a few years ago, at seventy-four. She had had twenty living children (twenty-one, when she counted her "love child"). Her daughter told me that her last words were, "Well, that's done now, and I'm proud that I kin still turn out a white wash!" She had just hung up her last wash from the "big house".

That was Sarah.

God was preparing me for working with animals on the goat farm.

Later, George and Bill offered to take me to the movies. We went and they kept coming back all summer to play horseshoes and just visit.

Niagara Falls

Poppa Boy (as I called Grandpa) was working as a traveling salesman for roofing material after his partner had committed suicide. One of his competitors owned the Ralston Paper Manufacturing Incorporated in Niagara Falls. He found out about Poppa Boy and offered him the position of manager in his plant. He was an Englishman and did not understand Polish or German. He knew his workers were ready to strike and hoped Grandpa could help him. So Grandpa Lee moved and brought Jim and I to live with him in Niagara Falls.

I think we went to Niagara Falls by car, perhaps Uncle Laurie drove us. I know we didn't go by bus or train – the only other ways to travel then. We lived with Poppa Boy and Grandma in the lower duplex. The falls were near enough that we could hear them and could look across the gorge to see Canada from the front sidewalk. There were three bedrooms, a living room, a dining room and a kitchen with a back yard. I do not remember anyone living upstairs, but there was an old Jewish couple next door that helped me a lot. We could walk to school. Poppa Boy worked at Ralston Paper Manufacturing Inc., also within walking distance.

Grandma's method of housekeeping differed from any place I'd been. She kept everything much cleaner. At first, I tried to clean everything as she did. Then, when I found out she was forgetful, I pretended I had done tasks and she did them over anyway – what a brat!

I hid sexy magazines under the mattress until I found that she turned the mattress every week. What a scene! Surprisingly Poppa Boy came to my rescue. "I will read every one," he said. "But then I will discuss each one with her. Then I will give her something else to read and we will discuss that each week." I could keep the magazines out of sight in my room. Those were some of the most interesting discussions I ever had with an adult. He explained in detail what each story was about and what they meant in the real world. He described what the outcome of the behavior would be and that "Good Housekeeping" outcomes were not the only outcomes from "boy meets girl." By the end of the semester, I was tired of the sexy magazines. I was much more interested in The Little Shepherd of the Hills, Treasure Island, Little Women, and other books he picked for me.

A Jehovah's Witness man met me at the door and walked me back into the living room one noon, quoting scripture. Poppa Boy came home, walked over to him and asked "What comes just before that passage?" The man couldn't say. "What comes just after?" he asked. The man still was silent. Then Poppa Boy told him, "It says in The Bible that there is no God." The man denied it. Poppa Boy said, "It says 'a fool hath said, there is no God,'" and showed him where the passage was. Putting his arm around him, he led him to the door and invited him to come back in the evening so they could have a good Bible session. The man never came back. Poppa Boy showed me how important it is to know the whole context of every passage.

Grandpa contacted Jimmy McWiggan, his former foreman, who was working in Detroit where grandpa had gotten him a job. He moved to Niagara Falls and took the job Grandpa offered. He and Grandpa met with an old Polish man in our dining room and learned enough Polish to talk to and listen to the workers. Jimmy spoke Pennsylvania Dutch, which is low German. Before they could work out the problems, one of the workers purposely set the factory on fire at noon one day. Grandpa and Jimmy worked to save lives and put out the fire. Both were injured.

Later the workers said that he proved he cared about them by rescuing people from the fire. They agreed to form a union to work out the problems. Grandpa took Jim and me to Buffalo to the union headquarters. They were amazed that the manager of a plant wanted the men to form a union, so they called the owner to be sure. Then they promised to send a Polish speaking man to the plant the next day. There was no more trouble.

Grandpa was very wise. One noon he came home for lunch and told us that a man had applied for work who said he never made a mistake. Grandma said, "You hired him didn't you?" "The last person I'd ever hire!" Grandpa said. "Everyone else would make his mistakes!" Later, I worked with a person like that! We were blamed for her mistakes!

He played the violin in the dining room with the door shut. I loved to listen to him. He had played in the symphony orchestra in Detroit. Grandma was a concert pianist too, he said, but she refused to play because her mother had been so cruel to her to get students for her to teach.

School in Niagara Falls was an adventure. My first day in 10th grade was ten days after school had started. My first class was English. I was assigned to a double seat beside a black boy. I refused and was sent to the office to receive a lecture on racial prejudice from the principal. I still refused. "I will not sit beside a boy!" I said. The principal laughed. "I never heard of a girl being prejudiced against a boy!" he said. "Where I came from the boys and girls were in separate sides of the room and had separate playgrounds," I explained. "Well not here. They are mixed up from Kindergarten up," he said. I finally agreed and returned to the classroom.

When I took my seat, the boy passed me a note. "I won't bother you!" He was William Roundtree from Mississippi. We became best friends and got an "E+" (the grades there were E, VG, G, P, VP. and

F) on a project for The Tale of Two Cities. We made a guillotine using a razor blade that was weighted at the top so that it cut the doll's head off. I made little dolls with red thread for necks and the little baskets for the heads to fall into. Years later, I saw William's picture in the center fold of Life magazine with the ambassador to Italy! His mother would have been so proud because she came north so he could have a better education than in the south.

The English teacher, Mr. Fabiano, had a Canadian accent. He helped William and me lose our southern accents. A Greek girl whose name was Yolanda Pelicano took first prize in the state for her autobiography, Thus Far, and I took second place for mine. Mr Fabiano said that he'd never had students take any state prizes before.

The Latin teacher, Mrs. Gratrick, was a very interesting teacher, too. She was an older woman who expected and won our respect. She taught second and third year Latin. I'd had first year in Sandy Springs High School in Brookeville. That teacher assigned and corrected lessons, but we never read aloud or discussed the lessons because he said we'd never use them. He read the newspaper to us. Under Mrs. Gratrick, we studied Roman history in 10th grade. A national election was going on and we were assigned to listen to the radio and tell her what method of campaigning the presidential contenders were using – Cicero's or Catalina's. She divided the class into two sections and kept a running tab on our scores in vocabulary tests. At the end of the year, she held a Roman banquet in the gym, with togas made of sheets for our clothes. I've never forgotten the

Latin she taught us, as so many of our English words contain Latin (as do Italian, French and Spanish).

I think that the Niagara Falls school system was the best I went to. At the end of the year, tests were given that were sent to the State Office of Education to be graded and then sent back. They were your final grades. I was told the teachers were also graded and had to go back to school if too many of their students failed or made low grades. I also learned things outside of school – how to ice skate! An Indian boy wanted to date me, but his father forbade it. He was the chief and would only allow his son to date Indian girls.

When George visited me in Niagara Falls, we went to American Falls and rode on the Maid of the Mist. We went behind Canadian Falls, which you can't do now because of a rock slide. The falls are most beautiful at night in the winter because the colored lights from Canada reflect off the ice on the falls and the ice on the trees on Goat Island.

During his visit, George took me to see his grandparents and uncles in Buffalo. They spoke German with a different accent than his mother's parents because, as they informed me, they came from Berlin. Later, one of his uncles came to Janesville to visit us. I also found out that George had a hole in his heart when I played tennis with him and he collapsed. In the emergency room, he told the doctors that he was not supposed to exert that much in the sun because he was born with the heart problem.

George invited me to a dance at the University of Virginia, where he was a student studying electrical engineering. I got permission to go after my grandma made arrangements with Aunt Verdie. The trip down and back was in a Pullman train. I got to sleep on an upper bunk for the first and last time in my life. I had to be chaperoned by Bill Muncaster, Eleanor's brother-in-law, who also went to University of Virginia, and I was to stay with a friend of Aunt Verdie's in Charlottesville.

At the dance, George did not dance. He ensured that I danced every dance except the first and last with his friends. During those, he walked me around the floor. I got permission to go up on skyline drive with him to see the sun come up the next morning. George arranged for me to meet his parents, too. I came down the stairs and fell at their feet! I was not used to high heels and shiny wooden steps. We went bowling while I visited him in Virginia, too. The ten pins were smaller than normal and so were the balls. We bowled our balls three times each frame, instead of the usual two.

Back in Niagara Falls, one Sunday afternoon I walked along the edge of the Niagara Gorge near our house. Suddenly, I heard a cat meow as if it was hurt. I looked over the edge and there was a kitten on a ledge below. I ran to my house, took the clothesline, tied it to a small tree growing near the edge, and went hand over hand to the ledge. I grabbed the kitten, put it under my shirt, and climbed to the top. To my dismay I found that the rope was too tight against the top rock and I could not grasp over it! The kitten was scratching me and yowling, so I had to go back down to the ledge.

I prayed as hard as I could for help. There was no one on the Canadian side to see me. Suddenly, I saw a serviceman's face looking down at me. The little tree the rope was tied to had been shaking so he came to investigate. First I climbed back up as high as I could get and threw the kitten to him. Then he laid on his stomach with his feet around the tree and I held onto his hands and arms as he pulled me the rest of the way up. What a quick answer to prayer!

Another time I saw a flock of Canadian geese committing suicide by floating over the falls. The survivors from the first round circled back up and went floating over the falls again. The geese kept going until there were no more. Some were rescued on the rocks below. School was let out for us to see them. No one ever explained why they did this!

I went to dances there with Jim, but we each had our own friends. I make intentional mistakes in math at first, because I thought I would be better accepted. I had been an A student before and found that I was teased because I got such good grades. Grandpa picked up my homework paper full of mistakes in math, put it down, and walked off. "I see you are cheating!" he said. I was furious. I told him why I hadn't scored well and he said "Years from now, you won't remember most of these students, but your chances of further education and jobs will suffer. You are cheating God, too. He gave you a good mind to use in His service. Do it!" I've always remembered that.

Grandfather went to Detroit to a party given by Henry Ford because as a young man he had worked with Grandfather. He took us on the shortest path between Buffalo and Detroit, right through Canada. We reentered America and had to go through customs at

Detroit. Canada was at war but America wasn't yet. The border had been tightened to prevent draft dodgers fleeing to the US from Canada and we were held up by the border patrol agents. My grandma was pulled from the car by an officer and her knee was bleeding. My grandpa was furious, but they wouldn't let us through because he didn't have a passport or birth certificate. I reminded him that we were to meet a lawyer friend, so Grandpa gave him a call. When he called back, he said that because grandpa was a Spanish American war veteran, he was automatically a citizen! Jim, Grandma, and I had been praying for help!

The last time I saw Grandpa alive was the day he went to Detroit on business. I was always glad I kissed him goodbye, as I usually didn't. He died in a hotel there. I received the phone call at 2 AM. He had left a number to call with me and Grandma, so I called the lawyer friend of his. Grandpa had been robbed and beaten in his hotel room. The lawyer made arrangements with the hotel for the body to be shipped to our house with no expense to us. He also had Grandpa's body embalmed before it was shipped. Grandma seemed like she was sleepwalking when the coffin was in our living room. I called my Aunt Virginia and she made arrangements to come. I notified Mr. Ralston at his plant, too.

People began to come to the house bringing food and comfort. People came from York, because Jimmy McWiggan called them. We found that grandpa had helped many people with jobs, education, and many acts of charity when he had lived in York. Grandma, however, went about greeting people as if she was dreaming. She told me that the man in the living room was a neighbor. I asked the elderly Jewish couple who lived next door for help and they asked if she was sleeping and eating all right. When I said yes, they told me to wait until my aunt came to tell her it was grandpa in the coffin. Then my mother came – drunk and loud. I kept her from Grandma and put her in my room with some food and water and locked the door. By the time she sobered up, Aunt Virginia was there and had taken charge. She told Grandma that Grandpa was dead and in the coffin. She opened it and left it open. Then Grandma cried and didn't sleep. The neighbors comforted us by affirming that she was acting normal now. Aunt Virginia made arrangements for the body to be buried in Arlington and took Grandma and Mother. Jim and I stayed in the house until they got back. The orthodox Jewish man who had sold grandpa his new suit, fitted it to Jim at no charge and refused the rest of the money owed to him. He said that he would not take money from a new widow.

I learned from Grandpa that each job, from the bottom to the top position, has its own responsibilities. All are important to produce the finished product, upon which all the workers depend. Therefore, all are important. Grandpa went from the bottom to ownership, back down to worker, then back up to assistant manager. Regardless of which role he was in, he saw himself as an essential part of the business. I later had a similar experience in my nursing career. I learned about grief and renewed respect and love for Jews. They have the same love for God and His Commandments that I do as they wait for the Messiah. They helped me to understand

Grandma's grief and the storekeeper gifted Jim with Grandpa's clothes. I also learned what a wonderful Christian man Grandpa had been.

Bryn Mawr

After Grandpa died, we moved to Bryn Mawr. Our house was a duplex with three bedrooms on a dead-end street near Aunt Ginny and Uncle Bob's house. Grandma recovered from Grandpa's death and devoted herself to caring for Jim and me.

I applied for a job as a child's caretaker in the home of a wealthy lawyer in Wynnewood, a suburb near Bryn Mawr, close to the High School I attended. The job was posted at the school. The child was called Bunny and her father was called Buddy. I lived with the family in an upstairs room next to Bunny. I had a connecting door to her room and an electric monitor, so I could hear her all-night long. She was four, a delightful child.

There was a black maid who was rather sullen around the child and I felt that the child feared her. One afternoon, I found Bunny hiding in the closet when I came home from school. She had red marks on her face and was crying. "She hit me!" Bunny said, referring to the maid. I told her mother who said she must have been naughty. When she told her father, he fired the maid. This made her mother very angry and she said I must do the maid's work until he found a new maid.

Fortunately, it was Friday and she had a maid from Buddy's family's home come until she found a permanent maid. It was then that I learned that the servants from Buddy's home did not like his wife. She had treated them badly when they had helped before and she frequently fired the servants or they quit. She was supposed to pay me every Saturday so I could give my grandma the money for rent, but she often went shopping with the money. Finally, I told Buddy and he paid me after that. Of course this angered her, so she cut the hours for the maid so she left when I got home from school. I had to do a maid's work plus care for Bunny. I didn't complain and made a game of it for Bunny.

One Friday, Buddy told us we were going to his family's home until Monday. His sister and her husband were coming home from Europe with their two sons. The parents had been arrested in France during the German occupation and had escaped to Switzerland where their children were in school. They had managed to get to Spain and then to the US. The parents were not well, so a nurse was hired to take care of them, but the boys were fine. When we got to the home in Philadelphia, I was treated like family by the grandparents. Bunny was taken to the nursery by two maids who were delighted with her.

I was seated at the dining table with the family – two brothers of Buddy and their wives (their children were in the nursery). Buddy's sister's two boys were with us as they were in their teens. I noticed that the boys whispered to each other and laughed quietly every once in a while. I overheard them whisper in foreign languages. Then the grandpa spoke to his wife and sons in French, and they responded in French. Then he spoke in Italian and they responded. Then in German. Then the grandpa looked at the boys and said "You are now excused from the table because you have very poor manners. You will eat in the nursery until I am sure you can behave properly." They tried to apologize, but he sent for servants to accompany them to the nursery.

Buddy was very considerate of the servants. Once, he noticed that a maid that usually went home early was serving supper instead of leaving it for me to serve. He got up from the table and took her home himself so her children would not be left alone.

When I was in a study hall during first period my first day at the Bryn Mawr high school, the teacher suddenly got up, walked to the door and told us to all leave the room. We found the hall full of students headed for the back of the school. It seemed that the principal had forbidden the students to have a bonfire with students from another rival school. The students were going to march to the other school and have the bonfire anyway. Some teachers had locked students in the rooms, but some students climbed out the windows. The principal was lifted onto student's shoulders. He persuaded them to pick larger boys and let him sit on two of them. He suggested the go to the other school by a back way so they would not be arrested or stop traffic. When the parade of rowdy students marched past my home, my brother and I went home. School was extended one day for this, but I admired the way the principal handled the rebellion.

The high school was excellent. Unfortunately, one teacher was very incompetent. He told filthy jokes in class. There were only two girls in class and the other girl laughed at his jokes. I left one day and sat on the steps. The principal saw me and asked why. I told him to go to the door of my classroom and listen. He did, and suspended the teacher. That teacher graded all papers that were typed with an "A" and all that weren't with a "C" or "D". I told the principal, and he then took over the class himself and had all the papers turned in to him to be graded again.

My brother was a genius in math. Two science teachers promised to send him to college if he brought his grades in English and social studies up. They said that he might be an idiot savant – only a genius in one thing. He told me that he'd show them he wasn't an idiot! He brought those grades up, but by the time he graduated a year later, the war had come to the US. He was drafted in spite of the polio damage in his back. The two teachers gave him letters saying he was a genius in math. The Navy sent him to the University of Pennsylvania, which he finished in one year. Then he was sent to MIT, while he worked on the first data processing equipment the Navy had. He left the Navy after the war ended. Later in his career he advanced to programming satellites.

My father came to my graduation, but he was very drunk, so I took him home and Jim got my diploma. Dad said he was sorry and left the next day. I thanked him for coming and so did Jim and Grandma.

After I graduated, my grandma received a letter from three of my uncles who were quite wealthy. They said that they had decided that I should go into nurses training in Baltimore. My Uncle Jim was chief of staff in the abdominal surgery department at John's Hopkins, but they said I had "bad blood" and wouldn't send me there. I was to go to Church Home and Infirmary down the street where Uncle Jim was also on the staff. Uncle Henry would pick me up in August. I was to have suitable clothes. The uncles would pay all expenses. They would also pay Grandma for Jim's care until he graduated. My grandma was angry about the "bad blood" but we supposed it was because my parents were alcoholics. My prayers had been answered and I had thought it was impossible! I had never told anyone that I wanted to be a nurse like Great Grandma Lee.

My journey in faith continued in Bryn Mawr. We went to an Episcopal church the first Sunday we were in Bryn Mawr. Since living in Brookeville, we had gone to a Protestant Episcopal church, but we had not gone to any instruction classes and still had not been baptized because we didn't have our parent's permission. This worried me, so we asked the pastor to baptize us after the service. He was puzzled, so he set up an appointment for us. After hearing our story, he agreed to see that we were instructed so we could be baptized. He assigned Father Moore, an assistant pastor who had been born in India to missionary parents and raised there, to guide us. The church was an Anglican Episcopal church, but we only found out later what the differences between denominations meant. Father Moore worked with us until Easter and then said we were ready to be baptized. The senior pastor was on vacation, so he made arrangements with the Bishop in Philadelphia. We went to confession before we went to be baptized. I felt very relieved after that and sure that we would be saved. The Bishop questioned us and baptized us privately.

Then the senior pastor interviewed us. When we revealed we did not believe in the doctrine of purgatory, he excommunicated us! Father Moore said it was not necessary for salvation because it was not in the Bible, but it was a teaching of the church. We were ordered to attend church, but not take communion until we accepted that teaching. He and Father Moore had a yelling match over our heads as we sat at the desk facing the senior pastor, with Father Moore behind us. Finally, the senior pastor said Father Moore would be sent to an Indian mission out west. He could no longer be in his church. How confused we were! Father Moore came to our home and reassured us that we were saved and explained the difference in the teachings in that church and the protestant church which the field mission followed. Father Moore's prayers had been answered because he wanted to go to the Indian Museum!

We did go to church regularly until I left to go to Baltimore. I talked to George about all this, and he said to contact the Missouri Synod Lutheran church when I got to Baltimore, which I did. The senior pastor also assured us that our baptism was valid, but we needed further instruction in the church's teachings. I prayed that I would understand the new teachings of the Lutheran church, but they had to be in the Bible, Grandpa had told me that there were many Christian churches that did not follow the Bible completely, like the Jehovah Witness. He thought the Quakers did, but were old fashioned. "Always follow the Bible," he told me and I have always followed that, after all, it is God's Word!

I learned that my prayers were answered for baptism and a chance for nurses training. I was right in refusing to listen to filthy language and reveal the unfair grading of physics papers. God solved that problem so poor students who didn't have typewriters could go to college with correct grades. I learned that there were differences in doctrine, but the Bible truths were not changed. Father Moore told me that the Missouri Lutheran Church was a basic Christian church that followed the Bible and would accept my baptism and Jim's so I looked forward to contacting them in Baltimore.

Baltimore

Uncle Henry came as promised and I said goodbye to Grandma and Jim, wondering when I would see them again. Church Home and Infirmary was located on a hill south of John's Hopkins, overlooking the wharf where ships from all over the world docked. There was a building where ships could be repaired, too. The first few streets had bars and houses of prostitution as well as hotels and warehouses. Prostitution was legal then, and the women had to be checked regularly for diseases. Then the next streets had homes of the sailors, many of them Polish. There was a Polish movie theater, too. Next were apartment houses and stores, then Church Home, then there were homes of black people from us to John's Hopkins. Then came the Jewish section and the highway, as I remember it. The city was west of us.

I met Miss Nash and Miss Eliot, the Nursing director and her assistant. Miss Nash was short and Miss Eliot was tall. I later sketched them as a toad and grasshopper and was disciplined, of course. I was taken to the dorm where I lived for the next year. There were four bunk beds in each room and one closet. I had one of the lower beds. From my roommates, I learned for the first time that people learned in different ways. I had a photographic memory – they did not. One student learned by writing it down; one had to hear it, then read it; and the other one studied it, then said it. I was fascinated and used this knowledge from then on to help others. I became first in my class and loved every minute of my training.

The hospital part had five floors with a cupola on the roof with a cross on top. Lightning often struck the cross and even started a fire one Ash Wednesday night. When I got to the hospital from Church service, there were fire trucks in the driveway, but no noise. We were told to dress immediately and go to the floor where we worked. I worked on the fifth floor. The elevator was filled with a cascade of water from the sprinkler system, so I ran up the stairs which also had water running down. Firemen instructed us not to go near a patient unless a fireman was with us and not to open any door.

The smoke was thick near the ceiling; the floor was wet with water coming from the sprinklers. First, we used wheelchairs to move patients that couldn't walk to the center of the building where the home for able bodied older women was located. The doors to that unit were usually off limits for us. From there, other staff moved them to safety. Then some patients were wrapped in sheets and we pulled them along the floor to the infirmary by crawling on our hands and knees. One student went too near a frantic patient in her bed and was almost smothered when the patient pulled her head into her chest trying to get up!

A fireman grabbed my hand and told me to follow him. He led me up the stairs to the roof and told me to go ahead of him and crawl through a window that opened onto the roof. I was to crawl along on the narrow wooden board that ran on the top of the roof to the cupola where the fire was. He would follow me with a water hose. He could not see the walk because of the searchlights below shone in his eyes but he could follow me because I had a white apron on that covered my back. I crawled toward the cupola until he ordered me to get off so he could turn the water on the fire. I slid down the roof, feeling for the metal cleats that kept snow from sliding off the roof, and worked my way back to safety. What an adventure! The fire was written up in the paper because no one was hurt and all but the fifth floor patients didn't even know there was a fire!

Every night we received patients in the emergency room from the 2AM "sweep" the police made of the alleys in the city. Most patients were drunk, but some had been injured or needed care. Drug abuse was another usual occurrence. One night we received on the ward a man we called "Joe" because no one knew his name. He was unconscious for two days. I was bathing him from a washbasin one morning, when I heard him say, "Are ya' busy where you're working, Sister?" I almost dropped the cloth. He had scars all over his body, a nose that had been broken as well as broken teeth and flat ears. It was assumed that he had been a prizefighter. He did not know his name either and answered to Joe.

While the authorities were trying to find some relatives, he stayed on the ward of forty men and was their favorite. One day, a limo drove up driven by a chauffeur. A woman in furs came to our ward, took one look at Joe, and cried, "Joe it's you!" and hugged him. He had been a Rhodes scholar who had been sent to England to school. He took a bet and got on a ship for the orient for fun and was never seen again. He was a boxer in school and in the orient. How God does work to unite families!

I was working on the night shift, doing charting in the kitchen, when a patient came in. He couldn't sleep and asked to sit a while. Looking closely at me, he asked, "Have you ever been to Hershey?" I told him yes and he said, "You used to go swimming at the pool there! I was the ticket taker and I remember you!" Then I remembered him, too. This was only one of many times God put me with people from many different places. It's a small world!

I felt so sorry for some of the prostitutes who were being cared for in the hospital, especially the ones that had agreed to be experimentally treated for syphilis. They were being given malaria in the hope that the high fever would kill the infection in the brain. I don't know if it worked, but some died. Before that, there was a lot of animosity between the prostitutes and the Polish patients in the women's 30 bed ward. We often had to pull the curtains around the bed or remove patients to private or semiprivate rooms to keep them safe. After these prostitutes came on the ward and suffered the high fevers from the syphilis treatment, the Polish women came to their rescue and helped the staff to treat them, especially when they found that many had been kidnapped.

A kidnapping ring that took young girls who came on buses or trains to find work was arrested. An old lady would meet them in the station and pretend to be sick and need help to go to the rest room. Then she would inject them with a drug and take them to a taxi, then to a house where they would be tied to a bed and made drug addicts. The kidnapping ring would then ship them to other places and sell them. When the ring was discovered, those girls who were found were pitiful. They were returned home after treatment. The pastor came to see them every day and worked to reunite them to their families.

Pearl Harbor came the first year I was in training. I'll never forget it. Our first floor had a chapel in the center where we met every morning for brief scripture reading, hymn and prayer. When we sang "O Holy Father strong to save whose hand doth rule the wind and wave, we pray for those in peril on the sea!" we couldn't finish. All the patients could hear us on the speakers on the floors and many patients were so upset they left without permission. Then there were the local blackouts and warnings. I found a man on the porch at night taking pictures of the harbor and called the police – he was arrested. The hospital windows were covered at night and we put flashlights in our apron fronts to do our rounds.

We loved to go to plays down town on nights off, but we were forbidden to go alone or to wear makeup. Of course we ignored that and met at the drug store, put on makeup and parted. When we met again we took off the makeup and returned. We were checked with Kleenex wipes to see if we had makeup. If a blackout occurred and we stayed out, we lost privileges. If we came in late, we were turned over to the police. "There may be many reasons, but there is no excuse!" was the rule, and it is so true! The rules were to keep us from being picked up as prostitutes. They should have told us!

One night I was cutting through the back alley coming home from seeing Macbeth, when I was suddenly thrown up against the brick wall of an apartment house by a large angry, black lady. "You are one of them little nurses ain't you? If something happened to you, you slip and fall or hurt yourself, all the black men in this place will suffer! Don't you dare to come down this alley again! Willie, come here and take this one home, Hear me?" A big black man came and guided me to the drug store to pick up my friend and then to the hospital. She was right, I never thought of the problems the black people had because of our behavior. It was a good lesson to learn!

I learned some lessons about different cultures, too. A young woman from China was admitted to deliver her baby. Her husband was a business man and had to go to New York the day after the baby was born. She spoke no English. When we took the baby to her to nurse, she took all the clothes off and cried and tried to prevent us from taking him back to the nursery. She stopped eating and cried. When her husband came back he went in to see her, then ran to the nursery and demanded to know what was wrong with his baby. He looked through the nursery window and yelled, "There is an epidemic! I must see the doctor!" We assured him all the babies were fine and he said, "Then why are they all wrapped in white? In my country it is the sign of death!" His baby went home in a little red lined black robe with a little black cap!

I also baptized a tiny orthodox Jewish baby, the first boy, at the order of the doctor because he didn't breathe as quickly as he should. The rabbi came after the family called him. He put his hand on my shoulder as I sat at the desk upset because of the family berating me. "A little water and a few words never will harm a little Jewish baby. They should have gone to Mount Sinai instead!" he said quietly.

The student nurses were not fed properly. We were not given enough Vitamin C, so we developed symptoms of scurvy. We were routinely sent to the dentist as part of our health care. I was the third student in the chair. When the dentist looked in my mouth, he asked how long my gums had been bleeding and I told him about three months and that one girl had lost a tooth because it was so loose. He took ten or eleven of us back to the hospital, charged into the Directors office with us. He ordered us to open our mouths to show her our bleeding gums. She said that we had reported it to her and that was the reason she had made the appointment a month early. All the rest of the staff had been given orange juice and fruit except the student nurses. They found out that our dishes had not been sterilized either because the kitchen staff did not have authorization to stay later. The newspaper made a big story of this. As a result, I lost my teeth before I was thirty and I'm sure the rest had problems, too.

I contacted the Lutheran church in Baltimore, and traveled there on the trolley whenever I could to meet with the pastor. He told me that he wasn't going to teach me using a catechism lesson. I would ask him questions and we would find the answer in the Bible, then he would ask me questions, and we would find answers in the Bible. When he was sure I understood what I needed to know and believed it, then he would allow me to take communion. I could also make a confession to him any time I needed to. We studied together until spring before he said he was satisfied. George was coming to visit me from Trinidad where he had been working, so we agreed I could take communion with him. I am so glad we did. He asked me to marry him and gave me a ring. I kept the ring next to the cross I wore around my neck.

The hospital hired many handicapped people; the elevator operators were in wheelchairs or seated on stools with their canes nearby; the switchboard operators were blind; the help on the floors were dwarves or midgets or had other deformities. The kitchen and laundry help were black. I didn't really notice this until much later, after I left, that it was part of the philosophy of the hospital – a visible statement of their Christian faith!

A big black man came into the emergency room claiming to have been bewitched. A Voodoo doctor in the islands had put a curse on him that he would die by midnight. The staff examined him and said he was fine and they couldn't help him. Then doctor Suarez Murias, from John's Hopkins' an intern scheduled in the ER, came in. He said "The man is right, we must find someone who can exorcize him. I will try, have him wait." He found a retired missionary and we gave them a room near the ER and put the man on a monitor that we could read in the ER. We could hear noises, but not words, cries occasionally, then silence. The blood pressure monitor was steady, then began to fall till we were ready to intervene, then it rose unevenly, then rose steadily until it was normal! He walked out a free man! The missionary was allowed to rest in the room as he was exhausted

Years later, I heard a doctor missionary to Madagascar relate how his belief that demonic possession was really undiagnosed mental illness, was challenged by a senior missionary. He said he witnessed exorcisms there as well as treating mental illnesses. God and the Devil are both alive and active in our world today!

My ring was seen by the supervisor in the ER. She advised me to hide the ring. I told her that many others were engaged. She said that the director would dismiss us. She hired only widows or single women and told us she was training nurses, not wives and mothers. I didn't want to break the engagement, so I went to the office in the morning. The Director told me that I needed to send the ring back and sign a contract to work there for three years unmarried as a proof. I refused and moved back to Bryn Mawr. I put in applications to continue training, but all were refused. I saw a letter the director wrote that said I was a "woman of questionable morals" I told George and decided to go to El Paso where he was stationed and be married. The nurse who was in charge of the dorm had told me to appeal to the board that I was first in my class and would finish at Hopkins anyway but I didn't believe her. She appealed on my behalf and won, but it was too late for me as I was pregnant. It helped some of the other students, though.

In Baltimore, I learned many nursing skills that I used all my life. I had opportunities to understand and appreciate many other people that I would not normally meet. I realized that they and I are all children of God and that he wants all of us to care for one another. I learned to show compassion to those who are suffering.

El Paso

I took the train in Richmond for El Paso. I don't remember changing trains, but I imagine I did. The train was air-conditioned, as it was in July, 1943. When I arrived at noon the temperature was above 110 degrees, I was informed later. The shock from leaving the air-conditioning and stepping into the Texas heat was too much for many people. There were paramedics and an ambulance ready to meet us! When I stepped out of the train, a man helped me down and then held me as I gasped for breath. In a few minutes, I could walk on my own. I saw men and women who collapsed and were taken to the ambulance or cars waiting for them.

I went into the station and called for a taxi to take me to the hotel where George had made arrangements for me to stay. He was to meet me at suppertime and we were to be married that night. When I unpacked, I realized that I had lost my hat! In those days, it was essential that I wear a hat in church. I had a white dress that I had made to wear. I asked the maid where I could find a store to buy the hat and she told me the stores were closing early because of the heat, but I could try. I walked to the nearest store, but it was closing. A janitor was just shutting the door. I begged him to let me in to buy the hat because I was getting married that night and he reluctantly opened the door. He turned on lights to the basement, showed me hats, took the money and wrote a note by the register. He shook his head and said he hoped he wouldn't get in trouble. I told him I would come back the next day and tell the manager how much I appreciated his help and I wrote a note, too.

I rushed back, got dressed and met George for supper on time. After supper, he called a cab to take us to the church. In those days, you sometimes had to ride with other people. We did. By the time we got to church, we saw the people who were our witnesses driving away, so we chased them, paid the extra fare and finally went into the church. The pastor was an elderly man who had been called from retirement because the younger pastor had gone to war. He wanted us to memorize the service, but we told him we couldn't. He made sure we had known each other for years, that we were both Missouri Synod Lutheran members and that parents approved. George's did. My grandma did, so he agreed to marry us.

The altar had electric candles. During the service, just as I was going to say my vows, the candles on my side of the altar went out and I giggled. The pastor frowned and shut his little book. When I was serious again, the service continued. I was so embarrassed! Our witnesses were Bill Roine and his wife Vivian. Bill was one of George's fellow officers – both were Lieutenants then. We were friends from then on. After the service, we went back to the hotel. We went to my room and drank some Coca-Cola but Bill had put some Mogen David liquor in it. I became so sleepy that I had to go to bed while they went down to the dance! I found out that I have a very low tolerance for alcohol!

George and I went to church at the early service the next morning. As we left the church and shook hands with the pastor, he held my hand and announced, "I didn't expect to see you at this service! This couple were just married here last night!" We were so embarrassed! We spent the day visiting with Bill and Viv at the hotel. We also walked in the park across the street where there were alligators. Then the men went back to the base.

That night I was wakened by loud roars coming from the park. I looked out the window to see a truck across the street with men forking something over the fence. The roars were from the alligators as they fought to catch what later I found out was meat. They had not been fed for several days because the caretaker was ill. They began to attack one another which alerted the police to get help for them. It was a beautiful moonlit night. Then I saw a naked woman walking down the middle of the street. The police saw her too and one officer took off his shirt and wrapped her in it before putting her in the squad car. Lady Godiva for sure!

The next morning I was called into the manager's office. He informed me that he had been informed that I had had a soldier in my room on Saturday night. He said he ran a decent hotel and that I had twenty four hours to find another place to live! I told him I had been married Saturday night. He asked to see the ring, but I didn't have it because George had taken it back to the base with him to have it resized for me. The manager just shook his head. He didn't believe me! Just then his phone rang. He started to listen, then looked at me and said that I was in his office and he would take me to the church right away. The pastor had forgotten to have me sign the wedding papers! Problem solved!

George found an apartment in town where we stayed until we were sent to Clarkesville, Tennessee. A dentist lived next door who asked me to write his bills for him, as his secretary was ill. So I did. I later met the dentist in Cape May, New Jersey.

One evening, I decided to take a walk in the desert. A little dog followed me. Suddenly I heard him whining. He was trembling, facing a sidewinder that was curled and ready to strike! I grabbed his hind leg and threw him toward town. The snake missed and I ran all the way home after the dog. The neighbor saw us and warned me never to walk in the desert in the evening, since that's when the snakes were hunting.

One afternoon, George and I decided to visit Juarez, Mexico. After some shopping we walked down a side street and found ourselves in an alley that was a dead end. Suddenly, a man looked at us and yelled "Gringo!" Then more people surrounded us yelling. My hair was pulled, George's uniform was torn, then stones were thrown at us as we huddled against a wall. Suddenly a little woman dressed in black ran in front of the crowd, yelled at them in Spanish, turned to us, pointed down the alley, and shouted "Vamoos!" We ran! We were held at the border and had to tell our story, then take officers to the alley and go to the hospital to be checked before we were allowed to leave the country. We were questioned at the US border too. They called the Mexican border people before they let us go home. We found out that a US soldier had been murdered in Mexico and that some men in that neighborhood had been arrested, so they were angry at US soldiers.

Clarksville

We rode a train to Dallas, Texas and stayed there for several hours. We went into the station. I called my Uncle Roger, who lived there. The butler answered the phone and put my Aunt Lucy on the phone. She said he was entertaining the governor and couldn't answer the phone. She wished me a safe trip and said she would tell him I called.

I had diarrhea, so I went to the corner drug store and asked the pharmacist for some paregoric. Big mistake! He said it was a controlled substance and I needed a doctor's order. I stood by the magazine rack while I had a very strong cramp. A Mexican man stood by me and whispered, "You got the bends?" When I said yes, he told me he knew where I could get some paregoric and to follow him.

We did, and went down a side street to a store that looked abandoned. He motioned us to go in while he looked over his shoulder to see if anyone watched us. Inside a man came from behind a curtain and asked me what I wanted after giving the man I came in with a nod. I said paregoric and he went behind the curtain and handed me a bottle wrapped in a brown paper. I paid him and asked if I had to sign anything. He looked startled and angry and came around the counter. George grabbed my arm and we ran to the station with him behind us. He watched us until the train pulled out. A doctor on the train tasted the drug and said it was pure. It helped me immensely! God was surely helping me again! I had been in a drug den again!

When we got to Clarksville, George and Bill were taken to the base and I went to the nearest hotel. It was full, but the clerk said I could sleep in his room at night since he worked the night shift and I had no place to stay. He only charged me five dollars a night. I found another army wife in the lobby who told me she would help me find a place. I went with her the next day to the Salvation Army where we rolled bandages for the soldiers overseas. The mayor's wife was there and asked me if my husband was an officer. I said yes, he was a lieutenant. She said I could live in her house and so could the other army wife. Blessed again! A week later, Vivian came too.

We volunteered at the local hospital, which was a mansion renovated to be a private hospital. The woman in charge was very strict and particular about the patients she took. Doctors had to pay her out of their own pockets before she admitted poor people. There were people who came from the hill country that she was especially mean to. I was crying one day at breakfast by myself when the black lady from the kitchen put her arm around me and asked me why. When I told her, she told me that the manager was from the hill country herself and she didn't want anyone to know. She said she kept her job by not telling and I must not tell either. I promised!

I told her I felt sick after eating and vomited. She asked when I had my last period and I told her November. It was March, so she put two and two together and told me I was pregnant!

George and Bill had to procure a shipment of arms for training. They needed a signature from the major they were under at the base, but they couldn't find him. They had been searching for three days and had been told he was at another base or back at their base. I told them I knew where he was and they laughed. He was in a private room at the hospital where I volunteered with a new young wife. There was a hospital on the base. They believed me and the next morning he was escorted out by soldiers. His wife yelled down to me that I looked just like Lena Horne, a famous black actress. I told her that I thought she was beautiful and thank you! The new colonel's wife introduced me to him at a supper as the little woman who had turned the major in! He was court-marshalled. I think he wanted to be.

While there, I volunteered to go with a public health nurse to visit some new mothers in the hill country. She asked me to take some baby clothes over the mountain to a new mother. I was riding my mule, when a man with a shotgun in his arms stepped out from behind a bush and asked where I was going. I told him and he said, "No you ain't," turned the mule around and slapped his rear. When I got back to the cabin, the nurse looked out the window and saw white smoke above the mountain. She told me that the still was running, so she would have to go. It was illegal.

I went to a tobacco auction. It was so fascinating to try to guess how the men were telling the auctioneer what they were bidding with gestures or facial expressions. The odor made me sick, though.

George was informed that he would be sent overseas soon and he knew I was too sick and weak to go home alone. He went AWOL, with knowledge of fellow officers, and went with me. He told me later that I almost followed another officer onto the wrong train while he was getting tickets! God was with me all the way. He told me that I came to see him leave, but I do not remember and it bothered me for a long time.

Back in Bryn Mawr

When I arrived in Bryn Mawr from Clarksville, I was pretty sick. Due to my pregnancy, I had been vomiting every day for several weeks. George had to go back the same night, as he was AWOL. My Uncle Bob was in the Navy and had been assigned to the Murmansk run to Russia. My brother, Jim, was also home from the Navy boot camp. Both were in Bryn Mawr to celebrate my grandma's birthday, but were leaving that night. My mother and grandmother were living in the four-room apartment that Aunt Jinny and Uncle Bob had made by remodeling their garage. It had a living room, bathroom, and two small bedrooms. The bathroom was a toilet and sink only. I shared a bedroom with Grandma.

Aunt Jinny had a roast chicken dinner with the trimmings and desert, using special food stamps because of the war. Unfortunately, my morning sickness got the best of me and I vomited everything I ate. I was put to bed. I do not remember George leaving, but the family and George told me that I went down to the station and kissed him goodbye. Many weeks of nausea followed, but I learned to keep enough food down to be more comfortable later.

I especially enjoyed spending time with Bobby and Jimmy, my little cousins. Bobby was about 10 or 11 and Jimmy was four or five, I think. I took Bobby to Philadelphia to see the Revolutionary War sites and to the movies. I drew some Indians for him one Saturday afternoon that I still have and gave a copy to him later. He had dyslexia which was not understood then, so he had a lot of trouble in school. He was very intelligent, but not being able to read was considered naughty and led to a lot of misplaced discipline. I read "Bomba the Jungle Boy" and other adventure stories to his little brother, but really for him to enjoy. Years later he showed me the copies of these stories he kept and told me how much he appreciated me reading them to him. His story will come later.

I will tell one story about Jimmy here. His father came home and complained that Jimmy looked like a girl with long hair. He was told he had to go to the barber shop and I volunteered to take him. The shop was about six blocks away, a narrow shop with the chairs for customers along one wall, and the barber chairs along the other wall. We sat quietly waiting our turn, when suddenly, Jimmy jumped up and ran out of the door! I called to him and ran as fast as I could being eight months pregnant.

When I arrived home Aunt Jinny, holding a crying Jimmy, demanded to know what the matter was. We reassured him until he was quiet. "I don't want to get cut, I don't want to get cooked, and I will not let them burn me!" he said and started crying again. I thought about what he said and then I got it! There was a man getting shaved with a straight razor that the barber sharpened on a strap, a man with a steaming towel over his face, waiting to be shaved, and last, a man who was having his hair singed with a lit taper! Needless to say, we had to cut Jimmy's hair ourselves.

There was a strange occurrence with their chow dog and the pet cat. A little neighborhood terrier was in the habit of running loose and killing cats on our block. Our animals were not tied and there was no fence, but they stayed in the yard. When this terrier was seen or heard, they came onto the porch and hid. One day, I noticed the cat had climbed up a tree in the front yard and to sit on a limb overlooking the yard. Our dog went down near the road. The little terrier ran toward him and he backed up until he was under the tree. The cat jumped on top of the terrier and began to tear his hair out while the chow chased him. Down the street they went until they were out of sight! I followed as best I could, when I saw both our animals walking toward me with no sign of injury. The cat had bloody claws though. We never saw the terrier again. How could they have coordinated their attack!?!

My mother was the department head of a small Pennsylvania Dutch department in Gimble's Department Store in Philadelphia. She had developed that department. She went out in the country and bought used furniture that was in barns or garages and had it repaired and refinished to fit into a home as an antique. The furniture sold very well and she drew and sold some pictures to compliment the furniture. The only trouble with my mother's work was that the department staff went out to eat before going home on Fridays. If my mother drank more than one drink, she became drunk and did not come home. Then we would get a call from a jail saying we had to come for her as she was lying on the street or had been in some trouble. I was the only one free to go, so I would locate her and bring her home. She was angry and sometimes almost combative and I would have to have help her onto the train, bus or taxi. I came to hate those trips and had no patience with her. She was not nice to anybody until she was sober and then she was sorry.

Grandma told me I needed to have more patience with her and that she couldn't help it – I didn't believe her. One day, Grandma asked me to go to a play with mother. "Porgy and Bess" was playing in Philadelphia. I was almost nine months pregnant and didn't want to go, but I did to please Grandma. I had the most wonderful time with my mother! The play was fabulous, with actors that were also in Hollywood, especially Sportin' Life and Porgy. I found a lot to enjoy with mother and began to see her as a friend. I still didn't understand her allergy to alcohol, but I did later.

My labor began after supper one night. I went to the hospital in Bryn Mawr and was left by myself in the labor room. I was left alone there for hours despite repeatedly ringing the bell and crying for help. Eventually I delivered Fred by myself. I was torn through to the rectum. I held him through the side rails, cleaned his little mouth out with the sheet, and got him to cry. Suddenly an intern came. He helped me onto a stretcher and took me to the delivery room where he transferred me and the baby onto the table. The doctor was on a stool but couldn't get up – he was too drunk. The nurse was not able to help either, but she told the intern a few things to do.

I got a contraction and the intern began to pull on the umbilical cord. When he said the placenta was coming out, I yelled at him to put his hand on the perineum and not pull until the next contraction. He did, and delivered the placenta safely. Then he cut the cord. I told him to call the lab for blood and the doctor did, too. The intern gave me the blood. The doctor tried to get up and the intern helped both him and the nurse out of the delivery room. Then the intern took me back to my room. He told me he didn't know how to repair my perineum as it was the first delivery he had been assigned to. A nurse came and took the baby to the nursery after putting a pad on me. That doctor didn't suture me before I left the hospital, saying that the next day was too late for a suture. What an experience! God was surely with me throughout the whole delivery! I was praying as hard as I could! It had consequences the rest of my life.

When I got home, I found that I had more breast milk than Fred could take. I heard that there was a Japanese baby whose mother had no milk and that they couldn't find another mother to feed him. He wasn't thriving on the formulas they were trying, so I called the hospital and offered to feed him. The mother brought him to me and I nursed him after I fed Fred, four times a day at first. Grandma was angry because he was Japanese and we were at war. How silly! Finally, he was able to suck from a bottle so I gave him his milk in bottles twice a day. He was able to switch to soy milk after three months.

After giving birth to Fred, I planned to move to Richmond to live with George's family at their request and George's.

Richmond

The Reuss home was a two-story house in a nice neighborhood. It had a nice yard in the back and a garden, a swing and a garage for the car. The address was 1413 Laburnum Ave. George's father was the church organist and his mother sang in the choir. George had a beautiful voice, too, when he was younger. They tell me that when he sang, "O Holy Night," there wasn't a dry eye in church. But then his voice changed and he did not sing in the choir any more.

George's father was also the principal of the Lutheran grade school at the time.

George's three sisters were living in Richmond when Fred and I were there. Matilda, who they called Tudy, was my age. Ruth was my brother's age and Martha, the youngest, was still in school as a teenager. When I saw how their closets were bulging with clothes, I understand why Mom wondered why I didn't have more luggage. However, I had all I needed. My Grandmother and I both sewed and I had clothes given to me. I wore the same size as my Grandmother and my Aunt Jinny so I borrowed clothes from them. I still feel that way – I have what I need.

Tudy was George's favorite sister and she became my favorite, too. She was a wonderful woman. Interestingly, she was least pretty one who later became the prettiest of the three sisters. She was considerate. As she matured she became very attractive. Ruth was very pretty. She was Mom's favorite. Tudy was Pop's favorite. Martha was loved by everybody. She was very talented in music and played the piano every day. She was lovely in every way. Tudy and Ruth worked in the city as secretaries.

I was told that the family had gone up to Buffalo years ago to see their grandparents. While Ruth was there, she had "pigged out" on food. She became a diabetic. She used her diabetes continually to get her way. I observed her behavior one Sunday when we sat in the front row at church. Ruth was angry because she couldn't get her way about something. She took some money out of the collection plate when it was passed. Then she got up and left the church through a side door. We found out that she went to a store and bought candy, which she ate. She became ill suddenly when we got home and was rushed to the hospital. Tudy told me she often did this to get her way!

While I was there, her doctor got sick of it. The doctor said if she deliberately put herself into a coma again from eating sugar, he would never take care of her again and she would have to find another doctor. The doctor told her mother on the phone, "She knows what she is supposed to do. She knows the amount of insulin she needs. If she doesn't do it, I'll never see her again." Ruth grabbed the phone from her mother and the doctor told her the same thing. So she did not do this again while I lived there.

Mom and Ruth teamed up in a lot of ways. Tudy kind of looked after me, but I didn't know the others were doing things behind my back. I did what Mom told me to do, helped with the housework and took care of Freddy. I also took walks with Pop at night. As we walked and talked I got to know him pretty well. I found out later that Mom didn't like that, but I had no inkling of that at the time. She was tired and didn't want to walk, but she did not like it that I did.

While there, George told about his childhood. He was born in Richmond, Virginia in 1920. His older brother was Carl, then Marie, then George, Tudy, Ruth and Martha. George was especially close to Mom, as Tudy told me. He was the family fix-it man. He also took care of the property. I think they had chickens at one time, too. He did well at school, but did not excel as Carl and Marie did. He was especially good in math. I found his old report cards in the top of his closet when I lived in his old room after Fred was born. From his story he did not do well, but his grades were mostly A's and B's – no F's.

He graduated from high school at 15. The college would not take him at that age, so he went to vocational school where he learned to be an electrician. As I understand it, he became the youngest electrician licensed in Virginia. During this time, he worked at Miller and Rhodes Department store repairing electrical appliances, including electric model train sets. The next year, he entered the University of Virginia preparing for a degree in electrical engineering.

I lived with them during the war and sometimes servicemen would come to church and were invited home to dinner. If one might be attracted to Tudy, immediately Ruth would make a play for him. Once she had him, she would drop him. I saw this happen three or four times. Then Tudy fell in love with a serviceman. She was determined that her sister would not take him. Ruth did it anyway. However, our city bus driver was interested in Tudy. They dated but she was afraid to bring him home. Finally, he became angry about it because he was really serious. When they were engaged and the relationship was "safe," she brought him home. Years later, he laughed about it and said, "I never did like Ruth anyway. I thought she was a mess. I was in love with Tudy all along."

One day I went downtown in Richmond at Christmastime. I was in the crowded department store and I found a pair of stockings I wanted. They only cost $1.50. I took them to the counter but then I saw the bus come. Without thinking, I just ran to the bus holding the stocking in one hand and the money to pay for them in the other. Then I felt a tap on my shoulder – an officer brought me back into the store to see the manager. The tears were flowing down my face. I cried, "But I had the money in my hand! I was not trying to steal anything!" They let me pay for the stockings and excused me and all was well.

We went to church regularly and then something happened. Pop lost his position as the church organist. There was some kind of problem there. He later quit the job as principal of the school, too, and went to work for a bakery. I wasn't privy to all the details and I didn't want to be. Pop said, "The truth will come out." Mom was saying, "No, you shouldn't accept this." He said, "No, when they find out what the truth is, God will let us know." I'll never forget that.

As it happened, the truth did come out. They did ask him to come back as organist which he did. He didn't come back as principal of the school. He was basically a very good Christian man who relied on the Lord. I really admired him. I told him, "I don't want to know all the details, but are you sure it's the Lord's will?" He said, "I'm positive. When people lie and do things they shouldn't, eventually it comes out and they have to suffer for it. I'm not suffering – I have another job. As far as I'm concerned, this is God's will."

Mom refused to go to church. Pop put his foot down. She was angry and wouldn't talk to some of the people in the church. He said, "You're sinning now. Remember that." So this was a lesson to me as well – to accept things, even when they were unfair.

One Wednesday night, Mom and Pop and I went to church. The two older girls weren't feeling well – they stayed home and took care of Freddy. He was in diapers and must have been about 8 or 9 months old. They had begun to change his poopy diaper. He was in a playpen in the living room with stool all over and having a wonderful time. He had stool squished in his hands, in his hair, all over everything. The girls were upstairs vomiting.

George's mother and father burst out laughing. Pop called up the steps, "When you have your babies, we're not coming to your house to change them!" Mom said, "You girls get down here and change this baby right now!" "We can't," and we'd hear them vomiting again. Pops said, "Let them alone for now." Then he turned to me and said, "From now on, every day they have to change the baby's diapers at least once. This is an experience they have to have." Years later, when they had their own children, I teased them about that incident.

I had not had Freddy baptized because I had not found a Missouri Lutheran Church in Bryn Mawr. I asked the pastor if he could baptize the baby. "Oh yes," he was more than willing to baptize Freddy so we made all the arrangements. I was accepted into the church, too. When I was in Baltimore, I had gone to the head of the church district there and had been confirmed there. They transferred my membership to Bethlehem Lutheran Church in Richmond.

A Trip to Columbus

I stayed in Richmond until spring. I noticed things were a little different toward me, but I didn't understand why. Mom told me that she had gotten a letter from her oldest son, Carl, a professor at a university in Ohio. His family wanted me to come visit them. Pop made all the arrangements and I went to visit them. They had two girls, 10 and 12. Carl's wife wanted them to see a little boy.

While I was there, Pop had a stroke. I got a tearful call from Tudy. She said I was forbidden to come back to Richmond and they wanted to know where to send all the baby's things. I said, "Why what have I done?" Tudy cried, saying, "You have done nothing. This is what Mom and Ruth want. They don't want you and the baby here. Pop was upset with Mom and Ruth about something that had to do with you and then had his stroke."

I then talked to Carl's wife, Thelma. She said Mom and Pop had come out to visit just before I did. Pops found out that Mom and Ruth were doing things that weren't nice to me. He was very upset and angry about it. Mom and Ruth thought I should be paying more to stay there. I had an income from George's service. The agreement was made between George and Pop as to how much money would be taken out of George's pay each month and I had done that. Tudy didn't think I should pay more. That was one of the reasons they didn't want me to come back. Pop blew up, I later found out, and was so angry that they were treating me this way, that he suddenly had a stroke. They blamed the stroke on me.

I didn't know what to do then. Carl and Thelma were very nice. They said I could stay with them, but there really wasn't room for me and the baby where they were living. Just then, I got a letter from Aunt Daisy, a relative of Bob Coyle's but actually no relative of mine. I had met her several times. She knew my husband was overseas and she had written to my aunt, wanting to know if I was available. She needed some help. She had broken her hip needed help during her recovery. In those days, they didn't repair hips like they do now. She had difficulty walking and could no longer go up and down the stairs.

Cape May

Aunt Daisy ran a boarding house in Cape May, New Jersey. She did have a little colored maid but she needed someone else, so if I could come with the baby that would be fine. But I couldn't stay with her because she didn't have room in the boarding house. Thankfully there was a house next door belonging to a Lutheran pastor. He offered to let me stay there. God again! Yes!

I had taken almost all of my belongings when I went out to Carl and Thelma's. I asked Mom and Ruth to send what little was still in their house to Cape May. At Aunt Daisy's elderly home, I made beds, did the wash, and ran errands for the elderly people and Aunt Daisy. I took the baby there, too, as I worked eight hour shifts all week except Sunday. While there, I made friends with the pastor and his wife and attended Bible study for the first time. Sunday school was in their house and I took the baby with me, since I was still nursing him.

One Sunday afternoon I decided to go swimming with the pastor and his wife at the beach. The beach was in a bay of the ocean. There had been an earthquake in the ocean some miles from the beach and the beaches along the coast had been warned, but the bay patrol had not been notified. The pastor's wife took care of Freddy on the beach while he and I went swimming.

While the pastor and I were swimming in deeper water beyond the breakers, we suddenly were pulled out toward the ocean. The rushing water pulled the sand out from under our feet and we saw a huge wave coming toward us with a small boat on top of the wave! "What can we do?" I yelled to the pastor. He yelled, "PRAY!" Then the wave crashed and we were carried toward the beach and the board walk. I do not know how many times I went back and forth until my bathing suit was caught and I was pulled up on the boardwalk. My skin was burned from being scraped across the sand and I was gasping and coughing up water. My eyes were burning, too, but I was alive! The pastor was, too!

We both said a heartfelt prayer to God for saving us. The pastor's wife had run up on the boardwalk with the baby when she saw the wave. We later found out that many people had been killed when they hit the pilings under the boardwalk or drowned. Many were injured, too. I give thanks now because the bathing suits worn then were larger and stronger than those worn now!

Shortly after that, George came home from Okinawa just after the atom bomb was dropped because his father had had a stroke. He had started overseas service in Hawaii, then Saipan, Tinian, then Okinawa. He said that he saw people celebrating the end of the war in Hawaii, but he didn't believe it until he saw the celebrations in Washington, DC. He went to Richmond as he was sent there and thought I was still there. I called Richmond when I got the message he was sent home, but Ruth answered and wouldn't let me talk to him. I went to the pastor and asked him to call. He talked to George and told him where we were.

Richmond Again

George came and took us to his home in Richmond. When we got there, George's mother asked us to find another place to live because the baby would be too disturbing to her husband. We rented a home in Hampton, a suburb of Richmond, and George visited his father every day. Tudy visited and told us we should be with the family, but George said it was better this way – less confusion while his father was recovering from his stroke.

Freddy didn't like his father to get near to me, especially to hug me. He pushed away from him, too. I said, "At least you know I didn't have anyone hugging me while you were gone!" Then Freddy got sick and I took him to the hospital. First he got meningitis, then encephalitis. He became semi-comatose and the doctor told me he was going to die.

I called George and he came to the hospital. The doctor told him that even if the baby survived, he would be a vegetable. George signed the papers to put the baby in an institution. I refused to sign. George said that Freddy was mine, then, and that was how he felt afterwards. He did help me with him, but could not relate to him well because he was retarded. We stayed there for a few months while Freddy recovered from the illness, but he was slow to develop in walking and talking. He had a club foot at birth, too, which I messaged daily. I got Freddy special shoes that were fixed to a board several hours every day and at night. He could not walk independently until he was three.

Hapeville

George was transferred to Hapeville, Georgia to be discharged from the army. When we got there, we stayed in a motel while we looked for an apartment to rent. George reported to the base and found out that he would need to stay there for at least a month, maybe more, before he could be discharged. We had no luck finding an apartment during the first week and were considering sending the baby and me back to Richmond on the train.

We decided to go to the little restaurant near the motel where we had been staying before we called the train station to arrange a ticket for Freddy and me and to call his parents. The owner of the restaurant had heard that we were looking for a place to stay and asked us if we would consider a trailer. We said, "Yes!" He told us that some gypsies told him they had a trailer to rent and gave us directions, so we moved that evening.

The trailer was across the street from the gypsies. There was a laundry house for everyone in the camp to use. One afternoon, I met a little black child, about nine or ten there. When the gypsy woman she came with went out to get another basket of clothes to wash, she began to beg me to help her. She said she had been taken from her mother in Mississippi. The woman came in and she continued to work with the clothes, not looking at me. I did my wash, then went to the office to call the police.

The manager told me that no one called Atlanta police without his permission and asked why I wanted to. When I told him about the kidnapping, he said that I was in Georgia and that any policeman I might contact could be a Klansman. If that were to happen the child would never see home. He said that if I would trust him, he would see that the child would be home safe in two weeks at the most. He asked me to bring George to see him that night and not to say anything to anybody. We agreed after he explained that the federal police were involved in something else concerning the gypsies. We followed his directions.

About a week later, he called us into his office and gave George $10. He was to go to the gypsies and offer to pay for the child to take care of Freddy for the night because we were going to the base for a party. If they agreed, we were to leave, but were to come back early and park at the office. We were to enter the trailer from the back so the gypsies would not see us. If they didn't agree, we were to tell him right away. They agreed.

The night was a beautiful moonlit night. Suddenly, George said he could see men under the trailer Then we heard someone knock on the gypsies door. No answer. Then there was aloud order for them to come out. No response. Then we smelled tear gas. It was horrible!! We closed the windows and still smelled it. We used wet towels over our eyes and noses. The arrests were made.

A black man came for the child, but she refused to go, still crying from the gas and excitement and clinging to me. We agreed to keep her with us until she was ready to go. The next day a black lady came and she went willingly after hugging us and the baby. The gypsies had brought some contraband across the state lines for the arrest, but kidnapping was not charged because we were told that the Klan would find out where the family lived and hurt them because the gypsies were arrested. The family was told to say the child had been visiting relatives in Georgia. While we were there, a cross was burned on Bald Mountain as a sign that Crawford Long had been released from prison. He was the head of the Klan. As we watched, some people cheered while others were sad.

Return to Richmond

George finally got his discharge papers and we headed for Richmond, towing the trailer. When we got there, we pulled into the family's driveway and parked. We lived in the trailer while we visited and waited for George's application for a job at the University of Valparaiso to be processed. I think it was only a few weeks. George's sister Marie was visiting with her baby Jimmy. She had been married in Richmond the same day George and I were married in El Paso. Jimmy was feeding himself and walking, but Fred could do neither. His club foot kept him from walking and he was developing slower otherwise as we expected.

One night while we were there, we heard the doorbell, and saw a Major in uniform who asked to see George. We invited him for supper. After the blessing, he asked how we felt about George's decoration, but we knew nothing about it. George asked to see him in the hall. Then we heard the door close and George came back alone. He said, "I don't want anyone to mention this again. I only did what any other soldier would do." Later he told me there was hand to hand fighting on the beach and he had to kill Japanese.

Valparaiso University accepted his application, so we left Richmond. On the way, we stopped at a hotel because George became very sick. His temperature was 104 degrees and he became delusional. I had to lock the door to keep him in the room. I called the doctor and he came, furious because we were calling him on Easter Sunday morning. I could hear him coming up the steps saying, "This is the third Sunday in a row I've been called here, and it's Easter Sunday, too! People think they can drink Saturday nights, and get drunk, and then get sick, and then they think they have to have a doctor see them!" He examined George and his whole demeanor changed. "This man is seriously ill," he said. He wanted to know if I wanted to take him to the hospital and I asked him if he could take care of him in this room. "I will try a new medicine called penicillin. If it works he can stay here, if not he will have to go to the hospital." I agreed. We stayed at the hotel for five days before George was well enough to drive us to Valparaiso. I could not drive at that time.

Valparaiso

When we arrived at the university, we met the president at his home on campus as arranged. He directed us to one of the dorms where we stayed until we found a cottage near the lake just outside of town. We sold the trailer for the down payment and enough money to buy furniture at the city dump. We lived on the money I had saved from his army salary and his discharge until he received his first pay from the university. I was pregnant with Tommy by then, and very nauseated as I had been with Freddy. I will describe our furniture when I tell you about the dream I had before Linda was born.

The house was on a hill so the back of the house was on stilts as was a wash house out back and another small cottage beside ours. Our property was enclosed with a white board fence. The other small cottage was empty then, but we rented it later to a couple who were students at the university. There was space for a garden as well as a lawn. The house had a living room, dining room and kitchen combined, a small bathroom with toilet and sink, and a bedroom at the back. There was a front porch, too.

George was a professor in the engineering department. He made friends with fellow professors Fred Krueger and Lenny Duval. Together they raised money to build a new classroom so the engineering department could be four years instead of two as it was when we came. They organized the students to help build it to save the university money and received recognition for this. Then George contacted Dr. Herman Hesse who had been his professor at the University of Virginia and persuaded him to head the new four-year department at the University of Valparaiso.

When it was time to deliver our second baby, the doctor asked me to come to the hospital and be induced. I went and was given medicine to start contractions, but was in the delivery room for an hour with no contractions. The doctor went downstairs for lunch, but less than five minutes after he left the baby turned. I had a contraction and the nurse had to step in and deliver Tommy. She didn't even have time to call for the doctor until after the baby was out, it happened so quickly! We had no insurance as the university offered none, so George took a job at the Power and Light company on the weekends and later drove a taxi some evenings to pay the hospital bills. Freddy and George were both allergic to the fumes from Gary Indiana's factories. Freddy was in and out of the hospital several times.

I became pregnant with Linda and was due to deliver her thirteen months after Tommy. Early one morning, when I was eight months pregnant, I had this dream:

> My Uncle Henry, who had a mansion in Maryland had died and left me the mansion only, not the estate. We loaded the red Ford pickup truck with all our furniture and headed for the mansion. When we got there, we went across the porch, through the white pillars, into the entrance hall. The curving staircase faced us. There had been a Persian rug at the foot of the stairs. I placed a hooked rug that I had made from stockings at the foot of the stairs. There had been a grandfather clock on the right wall. I placed an apple crate there with an alarm clock on top.
>
> We entered the living room through double glass doors and faced a marble fireplace on the opposite wall with empty bookcases on either side. The room was empty. I placed two candles and a vase on the mantle and a few books in the bookcases. I placed our sofa that had three legs and bricks for the fourth leg in front of the fireplace and our rocking chair beside the sofa. Two orange crates were placed on either side of the sofa. Then I went through double glass doors into the dining room. I was trying to center our white wooden kitchen table under the beautiful chandelier, when I woke up.

"We don't fit!" I cried. George woke up and asked "What doesn't fit?" I have always remembered to be content with what God has given me and where He has put me! Lesson learned!

My Grandma Lee came to be with me when I had the baby. One morning, I had diarrhea and then suddenly realized that I was having labor. I woke George and we headed for the hospital. On the way, George stopped to make arrangements with our neighbor for the garden to be plowed. I begged him to hurry, but it had taken so long to deliver Tommy that he thought he had plenty of time. He left me to walk up the front walk to the hospital. There was an old man with a cane walking there. I grabbed hold of the cane and we waited until a contraction ceased.

When I got into the hospital, they said there were no beds in the labor room. I saw a bed in the hall, so I climbed into it and held on to the bars at the head. A woman across the hall was yelling. There was a cleaning woman in her room. She looked at me, then ran to the nurses' station and yelled, "Pay no mind to the one that's yellin'. The one in the hall is having it!" The nurse came running, helped me onto a stretcher, pushed me into the elevator and then out to the hall by the labor room. By that time the baby was on the stretcher and the doctor was coming out of the labor room. Of course, he completed the delivery with no further trouble. God had given me three wonderful babies!

Grandma came just in time, too! She helped me care for all three, especially while I did the wash in the wash house. The machine was very different. It was large and round. The clothes were put in, the water was syphoned from the coal oil stove, then soap, then a large round cover with clamps was fastened down over the clothes. Then the container was turned on its side in a frame, and I had to turn a wheel in the middle of the container. The container was put back flat again to drain and the rinsing was done the same way.

George was told by his department head that he could not work outside of the University. Because we had large medical bills, I got a job at Continental Diamond Fiber Company in Valparaiso on the night shift. Because it was so soon after I delivered, I lost my breast milk. Linda was allergic to cow's milk and couldn't take soy milk either. She lost weight back to one pound over birth weight. A Chicago doctor suggested we try goat's milk.

George mentioned this in his class and a student said his grandma had a goat she wanted to get rid of. That's how we got "mean old nanny" a Toggenburg with long hair, horns, and a painfully large udder due to not having been milked for two days. Because she butted me, bit me, and kicked any milk container over, I finally had to tie her up right behind the house and milk her right into the baby's bottle. Linda slept quietly for many weeks. I waked her to see if she was OK and she went right back to sleep. From that time, she grew and regained lost weight. We then got a buck, too and nanny became very gentle. We got some angora rabbits and housed them in the cages on stilts we found in the wash house. I made a wooden table where I could stretch the rabbits out to cut and grade their wool to sell to a business in Utah.

One morning I was in the wash house getting ready to wash clothes when Grandma came running to tell me that a tornado was coming. She said we should take the children and go under the house. I said that we didn't live in Kansas where she had been in tornados when she was a child. She replied that Indiana had them, too, and warned me that I would never see the baby clothes again if I hung them up.

I did the wash and hung half of them up when Grandma called from under the house with the children and told me to look at the animals. The goats were staked out with chains and they were facing southwest and not eating. The rabbits were hiding in the back of their cages looking the same way. The sky was a lovely yellow. Then I saw the black tornado and heard the growing roar. I ran under the house.

Suddenly furniture came down from the sky and it got dark. The house shook and rain came pouring down. Finally, it passed, but we had to wade into the house while the rain poured down. I looked out the window and saw the goats swimming round their stakes. I swam out and pulled up their stakes and put them on the front porch.

Another family lived in the house at the top of the hill and now realized that the furniture in my back yard was theirs. I had seen them going towards home on the road in front of our house just before the tornado came. I found out later that the lady had threatened to leave her husband. He was angry and took them all down the hill on the other side to see the pastor. That is where they were when the tornado destroyed their house! She didn't leave and they reconciled.

With all the rain, the dam from the lake broke and flood water filled our yard for several weeks. George could not get home for a week and I couldn't go to work. Now we knew why the house was on stilts!

Working in Valparaiso

Grandma stayed with us about a year, while George and I worked. At Continental Diamond Fiber Company I was given a job of cleaning sheets of mica with a knife. The knife was wrapped with tape that was dirty and had brown streaks on it. Later I found out that it was dried blood from a woman who the workers thought the supervisor and his girlfriend had murdered. I held the sheet up over my head toward an overhead light to see bits of paper, hair, or other material imbedded in the sheet, then remove them with the knife.

I noticed that there was a row of outlets on the wall in front of us and suggested that the overhead lights be plugged into those with a sheet to cover the brown wall the size of the fiber sheet. The supervisor did this but he put a black sheet on the wall. I suggested using a white cardboard sheet that we used every 10 sheets we cleaned. He did this, too, and we were able to do a better job and do many more. He got a raise!

Then he moved me to another room with a machine that cut sheets as they rolled out. There was another lady sitting across from me who placed the sheets in a pile. She was the widow of a retired policeman who told me the story of the knife. She said that the woman who was murdered had attracted the attention of the supervisor and that his girlfriend was angry. One night she worked overtime when only the supervisor and his girlfriend were in the building. They said she fell on the knife. She warned me to never work overtime.

I noticed that the overhead water pipe was leaking drops of water on each sheet as it rolled out. I knew that the sheets were put together by a steam press after we cut them, so I told the supervisor. He said he didn't think it was enough to harm the sheets, but the next day the press was shut down. I suggested he fix the leak, but he just put a bucket under it. When the bucket filled up, he complained that the drops were still falling the same! Then they fixed the leak. My supervisor got a raise then, too, because he had told someone about the leak. Then he moved me from one machine to another and asked for suggestions. I did not have any.

Another situation happened that upset the supervisor, although I do not know why. I must explain that we actually worked the evening shift-they called it the night shift. We ended work at midnight, there was no night shift. I was given a ride to work by the husband of one of the other workers with two other workers. There was a union meeting that our shift was not notified of and the agreement affected our shift. We did not want it, so I went to the union headquarters in Gary, Indiana by bus and told them about it. When they found out that we weren't notified or had anyone from our shift at the meeting, I was taken back to the office of Continental Diamond Fiber in a limousine! There, they tore the agreement up and ordered another meeting where we would be represented.

After that, the supervisor had me work overtime one night by assigning me work upstairs that I couldn't finish on time. When I came down, he and his girlfriend were the only people there. I asked to call my husband but he said they would take me home. They just had to finish stacking some sheets from the press and asked if I could help his girlfriend. I stacked the sheets and she put sticks between them. We had them half stacked when he pushed me from behind and she hit the back of my head as I leaned forward.

The man who usually drove me home came back to get me when the others told him I was working overtime. He found me on the floor, unconscious with the two standing over me. They said I fainted. I had a bloody nose, too. I was taken to the hospital where they diagnosed me with a concussion from a blow on the back of my head.

While I was there, the president of the university came and told me that the department head should not have told George he couldn't work at other jobs. Many other instructors had other jobs because there was no insurance at that time. I never went back to work and George got his jobs back. I made a little money shearing my angora rabbits. Then a shipload of angora wool came from France and the factory I was selling the fur to went bankrupt. We ate the angora rabbits and kept the Champ d'Argents rabbits for their meat.

The school year was ending and George decided to buy the Cloverleaf Goat Dairy in Janesville, Wisconsin. We had been selling the goat milk and he found out that the goats there were registered and the sale of milk was profitable. He and Fred were still suffering from exposure to pollutants from the factories in Gary.

Janesville

We moved to Janesville in August of 1948. Fred was four, Tom two, and Linda just one. We arrived on a Saturday morning. We went to the bank to meet the Winships, paid for their farm, shook hands and left. We drove five miles west of Janesville on State Highway 11 to our five acre property.

When we arrived at the farm, we were greeted by loud "baaing" from the barn. When we opened the door, we found no hay or feed. The water tub was empty. We were in shock. George turned, looked across the road at the farm there, and said "We need help, let's go!" That's how we met Mr. Dooley and his family. We all pitched in – got a truck full of hay, bags of feed and watered all the animals. Mr. Dooley said that the Winships had left the farm on Friday morning! The chicken house was barren of feed and water, too.

When we entered the house, we found no bathroom. There was an outhouse across the long circular driveway to the garage, next to the chicken house. The goat barn was a long, low chicken house behind our house. Downstairs were a kitchen, bedroom and living room with a small entrance hall by the front door. This was not used, as the entrance from the driveway was up some stairs into the kitchen. There were steps up to the attic from the living room. The attic was one big room. At first George and I slept in the downstairs bedroom with the baby and the boys were in the attic. We later made a bathroom from the large bedroom, until we built a new house and rented that house. There was a large basement down from the driveway entrance with a water heater and furnace. I did the wash there and later made goat cheese there.

That was not the worst surprise we faced. George went to the Power and Light Company and found that the job promised him was not there. The man had not left as he said and the letter had not reached us. He called the university and they said he could be an assistant teacher there beginning in two weeks. Problem – I could not drive and we only had one truck. George could commute by bus, but I had to get a license! George taught me to drive as soon as the hay was cut the next day, by driving down the field and around bales of hay.

The drivers test was at the police station. An officer came into the room, looked at the assignment roster, turned and said "This is the third time I've caught this assignment!" in an angry voice. "Who's first?" It was me and I failed the first test – too cautious – but passed the next week with a different tester. Next remained the task of milking all the animals by myself, bottling the milk, and keeping the records. Caring for the children required keeping them with me safely in the barn. I made areas with hay bales and toys while I worked.

There were two gardens behind the chicken house, but they had been picked clean except for the root vegetables. We had potatoes, carrots and beets. I found out the Kroger grocery store threw away old vegetables on Saturday night. When I asked if I could pick them up they said yes. They thought they were for the goats, but I did not tell them that. I said I had just moved to the goat farm. I paid a small amount of money. I used the good vegetables for food for us and the rest for fertilizer in the garden. We collected this produce for many years.

George came home on Friday night the first week after he left for Valparaiso and told me that the job at the university was not possible. He had found a job on a farm near the university, but he came home to stay after a month because the work was too strenuous for his heart. I think he worked for Sprackling Products in Janesville then. He was finally able to work for Power and Light when the man left and the originally offered position opened up.

Mother called, asking if she and Bobby Coyle could come to live with us for a while. They were staying with Aunt Virginia who was moving to California, so she and Bobby wanted to stay with us. How wonderful! When they came, mother took care of the children and both helped with the chores. Bobby went to school except for the weekends. Then he got a job with Dr. Munn handling his ponies. God had solved that problem, which allowed me to go to Mercy Hospital and work as a nurse's aide.

Shortly after I began work at Mercy Hospital, the Director of Nurses, Sister Cor Marie, called me into her office. She informed me that she did not hire alcoholics until they had had satisfactory treatment. I told her that I did not drink at all. She told me that Mr. Winship had told her that I was an alcoholic. When I got home, George told me that his boss had told him the same thing. That day we received a letter from the goat registry that the Winships had sold many kids that were born after we bought the farm. They included the statement of the amount of money that the Winships owed us. George decided to confront them and threaten to sue them. They denied everything at first, but Mrs. Winship convinced her husband to go to our businesses and confess that he had lied in exchange for not suing them. He had hoped to pressure us into giving him back the farm.

I will tell a little more about the Winships here because the Lord worked in their lives and ours to teach us the rewards of being able to forgive with His help. Mr. Winship had had a stroke and was bedridden. Mrs. Winship called me and asked me to show her how to care for him. I went to their house at noon with permission from the hospital to bathe and exercise him. I was never on time, and never spent enough time according to him. Then he died and she went into a depression. I helped her get admitted to a mental hospital and she recovered and returned home. She called me and asked if she could use my house to meet up with a nice gentleman from her home town that she had dated before. Because a year had not passed since her husband had died, the neighbors might view her dating a new man with disapproval. She told me that her father had owed Mr. Winship money and that she had had to marry him for the debt. They met at our house until the year was up and then married and moved to Illinois. She wrote me and thanked us and said that she was happy for the first time in years. They both had accepted Jesus also.

The sale of milk that had been promised did not come and we were short of money. There were about thirty does and three bucks. The main buck was Duke, a five star buck. The others were his sons. There were only ten five star bucks in the national registry at that time, so we made money breeding him. Mother lived with us for several years. She loved the goats and trained them to pull carts that George made. They had races for children at the county fair several times. She was furious when we butchered a goat for food, but did not care about the chickens.

During the last year she lived with us, a neighbor was bringing her liquor from the tavern down the road. She was drunk when I came home from work. I found out that she could get drunk on only two drinks because she was allergic to alcohol. Mother refused to stop drinking, so we asked her to leave. We helped her get a car so she could head for California and Aunt Virginia. Her car broke down in Arizona, so she lived with the Indians and drew portraits that she sold. She made enough to afford car repairs and make the rest of the trip to California. There she lived with Grandma and Aunt Virginia's family until she married Ted Marchal.

Bobby did so well for Dr. Munn that he referred him to a ranch out in California when he left us the fall after he came. He had dyslexia which had caused him to be unable to read, though he could memorize very well. This condition was not understood then, so he finally gave up on school and learned how to capture and break horses on the ranch. He made it a career for himself. He met and married a teacher who helped him complete his education. Then he got a job with the county repairing roads in Oregon. I later met them in Oregon where they had moved with their children.

A farmer brought his stepson Byron to us in 1951 to work on the farm. He stayed for several years until he graduated from high school. While he was there, George worked nine to five during the day and I worked eleven at night to seven in the morning so that the children could be cared for. I slept when the children napped and before I went to work.

We remodeled the house several times. First we installed a bathroom downstairs using part of the bedroom and closet. We later enlarged the kitchen from the bedroom and turned the living room into a bedroom. After Marty was born in 1953, the tiny room with the front door was her room. The boys slept in the unheated attic. Later we installed a new furnace that heated the attic, too, so Linda moved upstairs.

I did the wash in the basement. Because I could not carry both Linda and the laundry upstairs and out to the yard, I made a harness for Linda and tied her to a tree so she could safely play with toys outside as I cleaned the clothes. Tom and Fred were with Byron in the barn. She untied herself and wandered into the corn field following a kitten. The corn was full grown then and when we missed her, it took many hours to find her. It started to rain and get dark. Byron took our little dog and found her three farms west near the tavern! She was soaked of course, but safe! This was the first time she was lost.

Summer Fairs

The next time Linda got lost was at the state fair the next year. We went to Rock County Fair and the state fair every year with the goats to show. I stayed there the week while George managed the children with Byron. We both took leave from our jobs for those weeks during the summer. I missed Linda when I was in the show ring early one morning. George and the boys were on one side in the bleachers and Byron was on the other. Each said she was with the other. I reported her loss to a sergeant at the office and asked him to notify the workers at the gates. He refused, saying that I would find her if I looked carefully.

I was furious and spent all that morning and afternoon searching for her with George and Byron. I went back to the office at three. While I watched the sergeant get ready to leave, a lady brought Linda to the office. She had a muddy area on her skirt where a truck had run over it – she was not hurt! She had fallen asleep under the truck. The lady was driving her truck and saw the truck backing over Linda's skirt, so she ran her truck behind that truck. The driver pulled forward when he saw the child, now crying. God saved Linda's life! The sergeant just walked off!

We took many prizes at the state fair, which helped sales of breeding stock. I watched a professional pickpocket work a crowd one day. I was standing with a police officer who had arrested him once years ago. He said after he had taken him to the police station and had him booked, the man had returned the officer's watch to him! The man turned and waved to me and the officer who said the man wouldn't have any money then, because he had already passed it to his accomplice.

I don't remember when I was at the fair last but in 1962 and 1963, I sold goat milk and sherbet there. We had a fair booth made of plywood. Some rowdies were shaking booths and yelling – having fun I guess. I refused to make any noise, so they didn't break my booth, but it scared me. I made the sherbet at night with the help of a deaf boy after everyone had left the dairy. They would not return until 6 AM. I put the cans of sherbet in the walk-in freezer. While I was rearranging the cans of ice cream and sherbet, I was in and out of the freezer quite a few times. I stayed a while as I arranged the last cans and when I tried to go out, the door had frozen shut. The moisture from my frequent exits had sealed me in!

To no avail, I pushed the door as hard as I could. I kicked the round knob attached to a rod that could be pushed to open the door. The deaf boy would not hear any pounding or alarms I could set off. It would be three more hours before the owner would arrive. I prayed over and over for God to help me. I opened my eyes and saw an ice cream can in front of me on the shelf. I pulled it off the shelf, put it on my front, and ran to the door. The knob moved, the door flew open, and I flew out to land on the floor! I fell down next to the table where the deaf boy was sleeping, his head down on the table. I had a big bruise on my abdomen, but I was alive! God saved me again!

Because I had had a concussion, I also had a period of amnesia one day at the fair. I was standing by the goat pens when I suddenly did not know who I was or where I was. I saw a cot and thought if I could lie down, I would be all right. I slept and when I woke up I remembered everything! When I got home, I called the doctor and he told me that it was amnesia which followed the skull fracture I had had after a fall following the birth of a baby that had died soon after I gave birth to him at home during a snowstorm. I was unconscious for three days after the fall, and had these periods for about a year afterwards. It was very frightening but later I knew how some people with Alzheimer's feel. God has His ways to help us understand others!

Goat Dairy

When we came to Janesville, we were able to bottle and sell milk that was not pasteurized, but only if it was all done only at the farm. The sales were much less than we had been told by the Winships. After we had been there for a while, the laws changed and we were required to pasteurize all the milk we sold. George built a pasteurizing plant of cement blocks next to the barn, then connected it to the barn later. We also bought a silo later. We sold milk in Janesville through Arbuthnot Dairy, in Edgerton through a store there, in Beloit through a store, and in Rockford through a dairy there. We delivered the milk ourselves.

We sold breeding stock to many missions overseas in Africa, South America, Mexico and some other places I don't remember. At Passover time, we sold kids from unregistered animals to Jews in Wisconsin and Illinois for their special Passover meal. In addition to Toggenburgs, which were registered, we had a few Nubians for milk with more fat. We had a little kid that had "H" on one side and when I turned him over, he had "I" on the other. International Harvester used it in an ad. We had a goat that was in two plays "Mr. Roberts" and "Tea House of the August Moon." Her name was Annie. She learned her cues so well that when the sailor was outside smoking and missed his cue to lead her up the steps onto the stage, she went on her own, stood by the ships rail, looked at the audience, and baaed. He came running after her and the audience laughed thinking it was part of the play. She also let all the animals out of their pens except the bucks several nights until I sat on a bale and watched her do it. I had scolded the children and had to apologize!

One other incident I remember was when Byron was with us. He had a shotgun he taught me to fire. One night when he was at a movie, I heard the goats making noise. When I went outside I saw a pack of wild dogs trying to make my does jump out of their outside pen on the north side of the barn. That was near me. I ran upstairs and got the gun. When I cocked it, the lead dog, that had been growling and creeping toward me, perked his ears up, jumped up and led the dogs all away! I later learned that they had killed many sheep and had bitten Mr. Dooley as he rode his tractor around a cow in the field. They also killed Mr. Dooley's own dog in his barn.

Harry Mull came to us from Dooley's farm. He crawled across the road and told us that Mr. Dooley would recommend him to work for us. His legs were badly infected, open and draining, so he could not stand long to care for the cows, but could care for the goats. He could and did. He slept in the attic with the boys and was with us for many years. He was there when Marty was born on September 1, 1953. He cried when I put her in his arms because he said no one had ever trusted him with a baby before.

With the help of the doctor and daily treatment his legs were healed. One day I was nursing Marty and Harry told me that he had known me before he crawled across the road. He said that I was like my grandfather. I asked him to tell me how he knew him. He said that I used to ride with grandpa in Pennsylvania while he sold roofing to farmers. We stopped at a grocery store on the road between Bird In Hand and Paradise on the old Lancaster Turnpike. My grandpa bought me licorice sticks. I called him Papa-Boy! He said he was the storekeeper! I did spend one summer with grandpa when I was living with Aunt Verdie.

At one time, George put up the dairy as collateral for a contract to deliver for Bowman Dairy in Chicago. We built the business to 2,000 quarts a day, then Bowman Dairy began to charge us thousands of dollars for shipments of spoiled milk. We had to lay off the two drivers. I was eight months pregnant, on leave from the hospital. Then George had a heart attack and was in the hospital. I went to the plant in Janesville, got in a truck and drove across the lot to a big Bowman Dairy truck to load my truck. The driver tasked me where the men were and I told him. He threw a case of milk down to me. It landed on my abdomen. I felt the pain, the baby convulsed in me and I fell to the ground. I crawled to the door of the plant. The manager hit my head when he opened the door. He heard the driver yelling again, "Send a man next time!"

The manager let me lie there while he called the ambulance. I asked him to call the two drivers for our route and they both came and ran the route. The baby was dead when I got to the emergency room. Then I was admitted. The next day, an attorney we knew came and told me that he was going to do something that was moral, but illegal. He was going to pay another attorney to plead our bankruptcy case in the court in Madison the next day.

He made arrangements for George and I to go to the court in an ambulance with a nurse. He had George's permission and needed mine. I gave it. The doctors agreed too. He was the attorney for Bowman Dairy and they were going to take everything we had on Monday. The court hearing was on Friday afternoon. We went and the judge took us in his office after we won and told us that we had grounds to prefer charges to them for the baby's death and expenses. George said no that he didn't believe in suits. We had to sell some animals and the car, but we kept the truck. We later found that the dealer in Rockford and another dealer in Lake Geneva lost everything they had because Bowman Dairy had overcharged them, too! Bowman Dairy went out of business some years later. God saved our livelihood! Tom remembers that Arbuthnot bottled and delivered our milk when he was in high school in 1963-64 and that George had delivered the milk to Edgerton and other places.

The dairy had folded by 1967. After the animals were sold, the pasteurizing plant and barn were torn down and buried in the field. The silo was sold to help finance Martha's expenses for her year in college in Frieburg, Germany. We had built a new house with a garage and rented the old house. We all worked together when we built the new house. The shell was put on the foundation but then George directed the rest. He did the wiring and plumbing with Tom's help and directed Linda and I with some of the taping and sealing. He did much of the woodwork I think with the boys. Someone else laid the floors. I learned to put the tiles on the roof. We built a metal barn to house a few goats and had room for a horse, some chickens and a pig. We tore down the chicken house and the old garage – the old outhouse had been torn down long ago.

When we sold the animals, Harry worked at a diner run by man who had been in prison. He was sick one night and I worked the night shift for him. I was the Director of Nurses at the Janesville City Health Department then. When I got home, Harry and George were waiting for me. They wanted to know how much money I made in tips. I told them that I had to give it to the boss. They were furious! The next night was Saturday. I did not work there. There was a riot – the fight broke windows and the police were called. I was so glad I wasn't there! Harry moved to an assisted living in Janesville and was supported by the county as his heart was so bad he was on disability.

One day Harry told me his real name was John Thren and that he had had a charge against him back in Pennsylvania. He said the charge had been dropped and he wanted to go live with his nephew. We called him and he said it was OK. He wanted to disappear here. I didn't think it was possible, but he said the place he was staying would rent his bed and pocket the money. He was right. I thought he would be reported as missing and I would have to tell where he was, but when I was informed that he had died in Pennsylvania, I went to the caseworker and he found out that his bed was paid for by a retired farmer and the county had paid for Harry's bed for two years! The place had other problems and was closed.

This will end the story of our goat dairy. I am sorry that I don't remember many things in order, but the experiences I had caring for the animals and being part of the dairy all helped all of us see God working in our lives. I needed Him many times as I faced hardship and danger but the balance of nature, birth and death and the ability to help others in the world through the goats and their milk He made possible. Because my actual career as a nurse began as a nurse's aide in Janesville, I will put my career as a nurse next. It was parallel to the story of the goat dairy.

My Career as a Nurse

I believe God prepared me to be a nurse from birth. I heard the story of my great grandmother delivering me when I was a small child. Then I had my little brother ill with polio and saw the loving care he received from the family. I took over when he came to live with me in Hagerstown with loving care, since the grown-ups had little time for us. He and Jackie Sargeant were the youngest boys in our "gang" so I looked after them through our many adventures. Finally we had to survive as conditions at home deteriorated. At Aunt Verdie's we were separated and had a chance to be independent of one another, which was good for both of us.

I had a chance to care for Edwin, Eleanor's baby by myself because she was ill after his birth for several months. I watched Sarah care for her many children. I learned how to love in spite of naughty behavior and how important loving discipline was in managing children. I learned that all races are the same in God's eyes because we all came from Adam and Eve – that the story of the black race was part of punishment going back to the beginning was not true and the way they were treated was very wrong. Jesus wants us to love everybody. I am thankful that I had the opportunity to have a close relationship with Sarah and her family, so I could help black people God put in my life later. Through the animals on the farm, I learned life and death and participated in births too. God's perfect balance in nature was apparent on the farm.

In Niagara Falls, I learned that the most important job is still a servant position as my grandfather taught me. As I went from student nurse, to nurse aide, to Licensed Practical Nurse, to Registered Nurse, to supervisor, to Director of Nurses, then assistant director to director to supervisor to staff nurse to supervisor again to staff nurse and finally to resident assistant, I was able to see that each was important as a nurse. The job description was different, but each job was nursing as God intended!

I have already described how I went into nurses training in 1941 at Church Home and Infirmary, now Church Home Hospital. There I learned the basics of caring for many conditions of illness affecting people of many races, ages, and economic situations. We served the wealthy in private rooms, and the street people in large wards. Many experiences there have been described in the chapter on Baltimore. The next experience in my nursing was as a volunteering with a public health nurse near Clarkesville, Tennessee.

When I came to Janesville in 1948, I went to work as a nursing assistant at Mercy Hospital soon after we arrived. I was assigned to work in the operating room where I worked for many years. I was sent to all the floors to fill in when they needed me and to the kitchen. I usually worked the day shift but sometimes was assigned to evening or night shifts.

One morning I was sent to the admission switchboard because the operator had had a sudden stroke. I was given a quick instruction to operate the switchboard and left alone. I had many calls that I got confused and finally pulled all the plugs and slowly reconnected the angry people correctly! I also connected the convent when they were on retreat. The priest called me and told me how to handle that after scolding me.

Then a man leaned on the desk. He had come from the entrance and was whispering, "I need help!" Then he collapsed on the floor. He had been holding his arm which had been amputated. I ran around the desk, pulled his belt off, and fastened it as tight as I could. Then I ran around the desk again and called the operating room. They saved the man's life! God was there!

Nursing assistants have the opportunity to work more closely with patients than RNs. I still believe that this is real nursing. RNs are necessary of course to evaluate and direct nursing care, but I think they should start as nursing assistants. Their training is for three years, and is important too.

It was when I was assisting in the operating room that I was given the opportunity to complete my nurses training. Dr. Munn was the surgeon and was completing the suturing after the operation. He looked at me and asked, "How would you like to finish your nurses training?" I was surprised and said, "I have four children." He replied, "Your mother-in-law can come to take care of them, but you have to take an exam to have your previous training accepted before you can continue your training. It is in two weeks here at Mercy." He also told me that the doctors and nuns would pay for my uniforms and books and all the arrangements for me to go to Chicago, Milwaukee, and Mendota, for communicable disease, pediatric care for the children and psychiatric training.

I really studied for that exam! I had Tom review me as I milked the goats, washed up and bottled the milk, did the dishes, and completed other chores! I passed! God laid out His plan. It was up to me to follow it! Marge's mother came to care for the children. She taught all but Fred to speak German. This prepared Martha for when she went to Frieberg as an exchange student – God's plan again!

Training Resumes

I took classes at Mercy until I was sent to Chicago to the TB Sanitarium there with my class. I do not remember how long we stayed there. I was impressed with how prejudiced the head nurse was against the black patients. She made them come to the nurse's station for their medicine, no matter how they felt. Some of them waited until the second shift came in to get relief! We were sent downtown to an area under the "L", near the Salvation Army to take medication, get sputum specimens, or take instructions to former patients. It was a very poor area. People lived in old hotels that had been made into beds for one night. We showed our ID at the door to a man who told us whether the patient was there for the night. If he was there he would be called to the door. If he wasn't, we had to go to another hotel or rooming house until we found him. One man I finally found in an old apartment house near the lake, but he had been dead for over a week. The next-door neighbor called the police and when the door was opened we found him lying near the door. It was in July and the odor was so strong that all of us gagged.

I found out later that the next class was not sent down to that area because a student was killed there. Her neck was slashed. I had never seen such poor living areas before. I went to the Salvation Army church and talked to some of the people there. One of my fellow students was a member of the Salvation Army. I really appreciated her friendship which I share to this day. I talked to men who had been saved there who continued to work with the men who came for food and medical care. God was at work everywhere!

We were sent to Milwaukee Children's Hospital next. This was the one program I had not completed when I was in training. I had had infant care when I had the delivery program. Since we were located near the center of the city, we had children from all areas, but most from the poorer area. All races were there. I found out that many of the black children were afraid of the white staff because they had never been close to white people before. One night a little black child was placed in an oxygen tent, but he was crying so hard it was not benefitting him. I picked him up and held him close, patting him on his back and stood by the window, singing softly to him. He quieted and then said, "You sounds like my Mammy, and you feels like my Mammy, but you aint my Mammy!" and he began to cry again, but not so hard. I got permission to stay with him until he fell asleep.

Another black boy was causing problems on the day shift. He was severely burned, especially his face, and was frightening the other children on purpose. He was 12 years old. The staff were angry with him as they protected the other children. He never touched them though. I found out that all the other children in his family had died in the fire. His parents blamed him for the fire and abandoned him at the hospital. Social services had not been able to find a foster home for him. I was assigned to him and found that he was interested in the circus that the children had been told was coming to town. The parade would be right in front of the hospital so they could see it. A few of the children would be taken to the circus in a special cab with staff. I finally got permission for him to go.

On the morning of the parade, the head nurse decided he could not go because one of the other children objected. He was devastated. Crying, then angry, he was given some medicine and he calmed down and went to sleep. I was sent to lunch. When I came back I found out that the person assigned to stay with him had left him alone. He pried the window bars apart somehow and jumped out. His room had been on the fourth floor and he died from the impact. I prayed that he was in heaven as Jesus said little children would be. He was such a loving little boy. He cried for his brothers and sisters that had died in the fire and his parents that blamed him, but he made me promise not to tell. His prospects in this world were not good. Caring for these children made me lonesome for mine, though I knew they were receiving loving care from their Granny Reuss.

Mendota

Mendota opened a whole new world for me. I had never knowingly encountered anyone who was mentally ill. We began with classes to orient us to this new world before we went onto the wards. I was fascinated to find that the patients were so normal and interesting! The purpose in writing about this training is to tell you about three experiences I had and one lecture I think you need to know. I will begin with the lecture.

The teacher was an aborigine doctor from the University of Wisconsin. He was originally from Australia of course. His family had been killed in a cattle stampede when he was two years old. The plantation owners adopted him and brought him to Madison with them. His adopted father was a medical doctor who encouraged him and financed him so that he became doctor, too. He specialized in psychiatry.

The purpose of the lecture was three-fold. Firstly, he was living proof that aborigines were not retarded – that got a laugh! The second part was to show us how religion rid the world of the threat of smallpox. A study was done that showed that the origin of most of the cases of smallpox was in India and South Africa. Further study showed that the Hindu religion had a goddess of smallpox. If a person got the disease and lived or died he would go to the next higher cast on the way to Nirvana, which is their version of heaven. So when someone got smallpox many people came to get it from them and brought their children, too.

Medical students from the university who were from India went back and convinced the Hindu priests that the vaccination for smallpox was the touch of the goddess because the sore was the same as the disease caused. Then the priests urged the people to be vaccinated and the disease left India. Then the students went to South Africa and convinced the Hindu priests there. By encouraging vaccination, they freed the world from smallpox! He said that the germ is kept alive in laboratories in America and England so they can make the vaccination if it breaks out anywhere. The third part was a lecture about Alzheimer's which was just being studied in depth at that time.

The first experience follows. I was assigned to accompany a group of patients to attend a movie in another building one evening. There were ten patients, one RN, and four students. It was a beautiful moonlit night on the way back to their building. Suddenly one of the patients began to sing, "Give me land, lots of land with starry skies above, don't fence me in!" Just then we came to the fence around their building and they paused, then all of us sang "Don't fence me in!" as the nurse unlocked the gate. One patient didn't see what was funny when we laughed.

The second experience concerned a fire alarm warning one night. We were asleep in our dorm, got up, dressed and got the keys ready to go to our assigned ward. I was the only student assigned to my ward on the third floor. I entered the building on the east side, ran up the steps to the east wing, and entered. An aide there told me to go back to the dorm that it must be a mistake as the building was fire proof. The alarm was still ringing so I said that I would be checked anyway to see if I followed our instructions. I went past him through the two doors to the middle hall. There were square windows in each door. Through the window into the hall I could see thick smoke and a body lying on the floor in front of the door to the west ward.

I got out my key, took a deep breath, opened the door, shut my eyes and ran to the door. I tripped over the body, but got the door unlocked and yelled for help to pull the man through. The aide from the ward heard me and we got him to the ward. He was breathing but unconscious. She called for help on the phone. He was the janitor, so she had to call the administrator also. He recovered in the hospital. It was the first fire in that building. It started in a barrel of waste in the hall near a chute for waste. The paint caught fire and the smoke was toxic, they said. My eyes burned and I coughed for a couple of days. I thank God I didn't go back to my dorm. He directed me!

The third experience was more serious. Within each ward there was an office where we met to get our assignments and help from the nurse and staff. There was a large room for patient activities and a hall leading to patient rooms. There was also a back hall where patients being discharged could wait for transport, usually only two or three rooms as I remember. I came on duty, went to the office, and was assigned to go to the back hall to escort a patient downstairs to his escort for home. As I passed the first room to go to the second room, a patient came out and grabbed me from behind. He was very tall so that my feet were off the ground and he was choking me. I began to fight and kick him.

I felt myself becoming unconscious. Then I heard a voice say, "Relax!" When I did, he shifted his hands around my neck enough for me to let out a loud squawk before I passed out. An aide in the activity room heard me and rescued me. I needed to go to the hospital as I had trouble breathing and a large bruise on my neck. It hurt to swallow, too. The patient had just choked his wife to death and was supposed to be admitted. He had been given a sedative and was unconscious, so against regulations an aide had put him in that room so he could go to report in the office. He was disciplined. I know the voice came from God. My training was completed there after taking some tests.

Public Health Nursing

When I came back from Mendota, I finished my time before graduation in the operating room. Then I took and passed the State Board exam and became a Registered Nurse. What a thrill it was to don the special cap and uniform! I started training in 1941 and although the law did not require this, I decided to work as an RN at Mercy Hospital for a year to show my appreciation for their enabling me to complete my nurse's training.

Then I took the position offered to me at the Janesville City Health Department. It was necessary for me to immediately start to work toward my certificate in Public Health Nursing at the University of Wisconsin. I received my certification in 1965.

At that time one of the responsibilities of public health nursing was to determine the needs of the community, organize the community to form a program to meet the needs, and then to move on. The first priority was to carry out the duties in the programs the department was running to promote the health of the community.

At that time, we had an immunization program for small pox and measles, a school program for vision and hearing and other health problems of children that were referred to us, and to work with the Sanitation Department, the police department and Rock County Social Services as necessary.

The city physician was Doctor Welch, Ida Hubbard was the supervisor of nurses, Mary Nolan, Eleanor Dewey, and Selma Weiskof were the other nurses in our department. Olga Fowler was our secretary. Joseph Lustig was the City Manager and Clifford Wanke was the City Sanitarian. I came to work with all of them in the twenty years I worked there and with the policemen, too.

The city had recently annexed an area on the south side of town that had some substandard houses. At that time there was no city ordinance to condemn property, so the state statutes were used when necessary by the sanitation department. I was assigned to the south side of the city. I had Lincoln School, Wilson School, St. Paul's School, St. John Vianney and St. Patrick's school. I substituted at all the schools as did the other nurses when necessary.

My first visit to Lincoln School was memorable in many ways. I came to know and appreciate a family that taught me many needed lessons in relating and respecting people who were coping with retardation and misunderstanding by the community and also a family who experienced racial prejudice. The principal of Lincoln School was Grace Knipp who had been there when it was a county school. She had helped the poor children by providing a noon meal from donations from farmers. Now they had school lunches like the rest of the city. She later was a Woman of the Year for the YWCA for her work in the community. She took me on a tour of the building after school and explained my duties.

After I left her, I walked to a door at the back of the school where two teachers were watching two children rolling a small child in the mud just outside the school grounds. They made no move to rescue the child or yell at them. Before walking away, one said, "The child is dirty and smelly anyway and they are not hurting her." The other one said, "They are not on school property so we can't stop them." I rushed out of the door and ran toward the children. When they saw me coming they ran away.

I helped the muddy child to get up. She was not crying she said, "We playing." I walked with her to her home. It was a small wooden house on a corner with an outhouse next to it. Her mother met us at the door, opened her arms for the child and comforted her. I told her what happened and she said it was not the first time. She invited me in. There were only two rooms. A large iron stove heated the house and cooked the meals. One window was boarded and there was only one other window, so the room was darkened. The floor was covered with a thick coating of old newspapers. There was a table and several chairs. There was a sink with a drain that went under the house. There was no water supply. A neighbor let them have two milk cans of water a week for all their needs! There was no electricity, either. I had been in cabins near Berkeley Springs as a child, so I knew many people lived like this, but they were clean and did not have the strange odor. I discussed the situation with my supervisor and she said I could work with the family to correct the problems.

Many visits later, I brought our truck and took the dirty newspapers off the floor, only to discover that the children got infected feet from the rotten boards. I got clean newspapers from the newspaper office to make a thick pad again! Lesson one! I took the board off the window and the glass fell out when the wall shook during a storm and cut one of the children. Lesson two! I found out that the strong odor that the family was noted for came from the solution they used when they cleaned the outhouse. They used it when they washed their clothes. The family that had given the two milk cans of water a week let them wash their clothes in their house for a fee. They also supplied two milk cans of water for cooking and drinking. The father was working on the night shift at the Chevrolet plant, so he had money to buy food and clothes. He had been giving money to other men who asked him as a way to earn friends. I finally began to listen to them as they told me what they were doing and why! It was a valuable lesson.

The parents told me that they were concerned that the children had not been baptized. They had been told by their parents that they would not be accepted by either protestant or catholic churches because the wife was catholic and the husband was protestant. They had been married by the Justice of the Peace. On my regular visit to St. Patrick's school, I told Father MacNamara. He welcomed them into his church and baptized the father and all the children.

The house was condemned, of course, but no other place would allow them to rent. This created the first community need that I began to work on – the Low Cost Housing program. In the next section I will tell about how this came about, but now I will follow the family from this house to the next.

Rock County Social Services informed my supervisor that they were going to court to take the children because of the living conditions. When I told Father MacNamara what the social services was doing, he got a retired missionary from his church to testify in court that thousands of people live the way they did. Their family doctor testified they were healthy and their diet was adequate. They had fruit and cold cereal in the morning and meat and vegetables in the large pot for noon and supper. There had been no reports of mistreatment of the children. They were allowed to keep the children.

While the new house was built, a family allowed them to stay in a remodeled garage. There was a shower, but no tub. They proudly showed me that they had found an old wire in the dump and placed it in the shower so that they could be sure the children were clean. The wire was old and the covering was off in places. I removed it and told them to use the wash tub in the kitchen instead. I did not tell them then it was so dangerous because they were so proud of solving the problem. While I was there, a milkman persuaded the mother to pay the kind neighbor's milk bill. I found his truck at the tavern where he was sitting drinking beer. I asked the bartender to use the phone, called the dairy owner and explained the situation. Needless to say, her money was returned!

The children went to a different grade school because of the move. They moved into the new cement block house and began to get used to their new neighborhood. The oldest son had joined the army and was stationed in Germany. He sent for his parents to visit. They were thrilled! A relative went with them to buy clothes and made all arrangements for the trip! It remained the highlight of their life. However several teachers at the new school thought it was a waste of money. I was angry and said so to them. I later apologized and explained what it meant to them. Later, the government 235 housing program came and they moved again into one of those houses. They had several more children. When they moved into the new house it meant changing schools again. This time the second oldest girl was left alone in the classroom all day because her father had not paid for her ticket to go on a school trip on Wednesday. He had had to wait until his payday on Friday to paid for the ticket. The School Superintendent went with me to the principal and told her that all the children were to go – even those who could not pay.

Three of the children in the family were retarded. One of the three died, one married and one is in Kandu now. The normal children are married and responsible members of society. The parents are dead now and the second oldest daughter keeps in touch with the rest. She has a summer picnic that I am invited to.

It was obvious to me that God was working with this family, as their most pressing concern in the beginning was for their return to church. Their love and support of each other still is shown. There was no resentment expressed toward others when they were mistreated. Through their church's actions and the support of their doctor they were able to keep their children.

The second family that I met at Lincoln School that was persecuted was the family of an Indian man who had married a white woman. He was a decorated war veteran who had purchased land near the school and built a house there. I was told that the house had been burned down and a sign was placed there with "We Don't Want Indians Here!" written on it. He had bought a trailer and put a lean-to on it. They had two children, I believe. Those children defended themselves and caused no problem I was told. He wanted to use the property as collateral to buy a house, but no one would sell to him without a loan. He worked for a roofing company.

He took me with him when he went to a bank one Saturday, because he wanted me to see if he could get a loan. The manager took me aside and said that he never gave loans to Indians, especially as he had married a white woman. We went to his boss then His boss went with us to the bank and took all his money for his business and personal property out of that bank and went to another bank and deposited it. Then the boss bought a house, accepted the Indian's collateral, and made arrangements for him to repay him out of his paycheck. The family had no problems in the new neighborhood, they told me. God moved the boss to make it possible for the Indian family to move to a new neighborhood where they would be better off. He showed love and compassion.

Janesville was a Klan town when we moved there. There were two black families. One was a retired Pullman railroad worker and his wife on the south side and the other was a family with several children on the west side. When the teenage boy broke his leg, Mercy Hospital had to change the nursing staff to care for him. No black people were hired except at the Chevrolet Plant where it was required. Then Geraldo, a newsman, came and confronted the Klan leader. He was attacked and injured and had to be treated in Mercy Hospital. The media picked it up and the churches woke up and began to influence their people to stop discrimination. People from Vietnam began to come with church sponsorship. The laws for housing and work changed and now it is finally integrated. God wants us all to be brothers and sisters!

Before there was a visiting nurse organization, we were called to help bathe and teach families to care for ill family members in their home. I had just helped his wife to assist an elderly man into his bath tub, when a little girl came running up the stairs yelling "Nurse, come quick! My mother is choking my baby sister, she's crazy!" I left the man after telling his wife to keep the water warm and get a bathrobe to keep him warm in the tub. She urged me to hurry, that she knew the neighbor had been in the mental hospital.

Bursting into the house next door, I was confronted with a hysterical woman waving a butcher knife who screamed at me, slammed the door and locked it "The aliens are here! Help me fight them! The baby turns into one until I choke her, then she turns into a baby again!" There was broken glass on the floor, debris everywhere. I reached for the phone on the wall, she screamed "Don't touch it! It is activated. If you touch it you will turn into an alien and I'll have to kill you!" I said a quick prayer and said "This little pin on my cap will deactivate the phone and I can call for help, I'll show you."

I touched the PHN pin on my cap and I grabbed the phone and called the police department while she held the knife at my throat. I was connected to an officer I knew well. "This is Mary Lee Reuss, I am calling from (I gave the address). We are being invaded by aliens and need help right away. Please send Inspector Chicks to help us fight them!" (He was actually Dr. Chicks a psychiatrist) After a brief pause he said "Dr. Chicks?" "Yes," I said, "Right away!" She moved the knife away from my throat, but kept it in her hand, watching me closely. She began to pace, and cry, starting at every sound. The baby was whimpering and had red marks on her throat, but was breathing all right. She was holding onto her big sister on the sofa.

After what seemed like a long time, but really wasn't, the police arrived with Dr. Chicks. I unlocked the door after touching my pin as the woman threatened me again. The policemen held the lady while she struggled and the doctor gave her an injection while assuring her that she would be all right. She finally relaxed and seemed to recognize Dr. Chicks. Then she hugged him and went willingly back to the mental hospital in the police car after telling me to take care of the children and to be careful of the aliens.

I called Social Services and waited for them to come for the children, then returned to my patient in the tub. He was warm and we were all thankful that it had turned out well. We finished his care and then prayed for the little family before I left. I apologized for not calling my supervisor to send someone to help them while I waited for Social Services to take the children. I had a red mark from the knife on my throat! The thought to touch my pin came from God!

While I was a public health nurse I had been working with a young wife of a Vietnam veteran who had a 2-year-old child and a 3-month-old baby. The baby had been diagnosed with PKU, which necessitated that she be fed a special formula to prevent her from becoming brain damaged. The doctor was concerned because the mother had epilepsy and was not under good control. I made frequent visits to monitor the baby's condition and the mother's ability to feed the baby correctly. The mother seemed confused – she was still feeding the older child with a bottle and although I had marked the baby's bottle with a red sticker, she confused the bottles several times. I reported this and the doctor had arranged with social services to go to court to remove the baby from the home. I would need to testify the next day.

The mother had several seizures during my visits and was confused afterwards. I made the last visit to inform the mother that the baby needed to be placed in a foster home but that she would have regular visits to see her, and that I would continue to visit her and the older child while the doctor worked to control her seizures.

While I was there, her husband arrived. He was being discharged from the army and had not been home when I had visited before. I explained the situation to them both. He suddenly got up and stood by the only door out of the second-floor apartment. He drew a switchblade and threatened to kill me if I testified in court to remove the baby. I prayed for the right words to say. I felt calm then. "What will you do with my body? The only way out is an open stairs in plain view of the street. The health department knows I'm here. There will be blood everywhere. You will go to prison and the baby will still be removed to save her life." He stood still, then yelled "Get out!!" I walked past him, then ran down the steps to my car!

The baby was placed with the grandmother in Illinois. She took the mother and older child and the husband, too. She agreed to a referral to a doctor in her city to care for the mother and children with supervision from the health dept in her city.

Three years later, the veteran came to my office with a newborn baby to thank me. He said he was so angry that he wanted to kill me that day. He said that his former wife was in a mental hospital and did not know anyone. She had many seizures every day. He had a divorce and had married his childhood sweetheart. This was his new baby. The other baby was fine, and she and her sister lived with them. They saw grandmother every week, when he took the children to see their mother. She was not expected to live much longer. He and his new wife both hugged me! I told them to thank God who gave me the words to say!

Community Programs

Because safe housing is an essential part of community health, and because the area I was assigned to had many examples of poor housing, I worked closely with the city sanitation department manager, Clifford Wanke. Here are some examples of unhealthy situations I encountered:

> A basement apartment was flooded for many months, requiring the tenants to wear boots. There were three children under ten living there with their parents.
>
> An upstairs apartment had a sagging ceiling that broke, hurting a child in his crib below. It was not repaired even though pieces kept falling so I finally took a broom and finished breaking the ceiling. Even then it was not repaired.
>
> An apartment had sewage leaking through the ceiling from a toilet above. The residents kept a bucket under the leak to catch the sewage.
>
> Apartments with broken or lacking stair treads, broken windows, unsafe electrical wiring, etc., etc., etc.

At that time, the city had no housing code, so the state condemnation laws had to be used. I notified Cliff and he issued the condemnations. This required the tenants to move in two weeks or be fined, but the landlord was not fined. A notice was posted on the building and it was not supposed to be rented again until it met the building requirements. Often the notice was simply removed and the place rented again. When I found out, I called Cliff and he recondemned the place. The landlord was not fined.

Cliff finally photographed the places, took the pictures to the city council and explained why he needed a city building code. He did not get one. Someone told him that the landlords of some of the condemned buildings were on the city council! The YWCA displayed the pictures in their office. Some years later, the city did get a building code because they needed one to renovate the downtown area. Then a building inspector was given an office. We reported to him after we found other places for the tenants to rent. Problem solved!

Since my area had many poor people, people gave me clothes for them. There were several large families on one corner who offered to wash and label sizes on the clothes. I gave them out as needed from the back of my city car. Mrs. Knipp referred the families in need to me.

One day Laura Jakobek, who lived in the area, offered to take the clothes to St. Patrick's church to be given out. She said that Father MacNamara had suggested that they would do that. I agreed. The church formed an organization called Every Catholic Helps Others or ECHO. They would help all the people. Soon the organization was called Every Christian Helps Others because other churches wanted to join. Then it became Every Citizen Helps Others because other groups wanted to join.

Now it is called Every Community Helps Others because it serves five communities the last I heard. Food, clothes and other donations are sent out in vans or picked up there. They have other services to help people too! How wonderful God is to make a program to help people grow like this!!!

Community Action and its program, Head Start began in Beloit. There was an article in the Janesville Gazette written by a women's group that said that we did not need the program in Janesville. Father Perek from St. Mary's church asked Ida Hubbard to send me to Beloit to work with Community Action to see if the program could be brought to Janesville. He had many in his congregation that could benefit and so did the other churches. I agreed to go on my own time and was accepted on the board as it was a county organization.

Head Start in Janesville started at the Congregational Church. I visited there to check the vision of the children. A group of ladies came in, looked at the teacher and children, turned and walked out without speaking. I followed them because I was finished and heard one say, "I told you we didn't need that program. I didn't see any dirty or ragged children, did you?" I told them that I knew the families and they were poor, but they kept their children clean and in the best clothes they had. They got in their car and drove away. Head Start has been a blessing for many children. Community Action eventually moved to Janesville. I remained on the board for many years.

I also helped develop the sheltered workshop, which is now called Kandu. Mary Hopkins was a member of the Association for Retarded Children which I belonged to also. Kennedy was President and his party became interested in retardation as his sister was at St.

Colletta's, a home for retarded people. A program for retarded children had begun in the Janesville school system. I enrolled my son, Fred, in the Junior High program. He was the first to come from a country school.

Mary became concerned about the young retarded adults who had no programs or services, so she began a program in her living room. She taught them some crafts, and helped improve their reading, writing, and arithmetic. She focused on teaching practical skills for living and relating to someone other than parents or relatives.

Sheltered workshops were being talked about and a board was formed which I belonged to. A school for trainable level retarded children was dedicated near the Rock County Home and Mental Hospital. The Vice President's wife, Muriel Humphrey, came to dedicate it. I was the Director of Nurses at the Janesville City Health Department, as Ida Hubbard had retired. The City Manager, Mr. Lustig, asked me to meet Mrs. Humphrey and escort her to a banquet where she was to dedicate the new school.

My new dress for the banquet was donated by Mr. Eliot from his store in Fort Atkinson. His staff in Janesville would not wait on me in barn clothes! I met Mrs. Humphrey at the hotel. We were in a limousine, of course. All the traffic lights were green all the way to the banquet and back. We had a police escort, too, ahead and behind us. She was a fascinating lady, very gracious, but human, too, noting humorous things on the way. The program at the banquet was arranged by the ARC to include some of the retarded children. Mr.

Lustig donated a vacant public school to become the first sheltered workshop! We had not expected that!

The first contract we had was from Parker Pen. It was an advertising flyer to be assembled and packaged. Because the few workers could not complete it on time at first, my husband picked up the unfinished work on Friday night and delivered it to each worker for them to do at their home. He picked it up on Sunday night for the workshop on Monday morning. Soon more workers came, their skills improved, and they were able to complete the work on time.

The sheltered workshop later moved to a new building on Kellog Avenue where it continued to grow. The name was changed to Kandu. I remained on the board until I moved to Stoughton the first time.

I received an award for my community service as woman of the year from Janesville YWCA. I also was an office in the local and national association for retarded children.

Caravilla

The Janesville Public Health Department was incorporated with the County Public Health Department. I was offered a position but decided to take the position of Assistant Director of Nursing at Caravilla Nursing Home. It was located between Janesville and Beloit on a very large lot. John Falko was the Administrator and Rona Dolgner was the director of Nurses. I had to learn to manage a number of staff and of course all the laws concerning the residents.

Shortly after I came, my mother and her husband called, they were in a nursing home in California. They were not allowed to see each other except for two hours on a Saturday afternoon. I flew out and brought both of them in wheel chairs to live together in one room in Caravilla. They lived there for two years, enjoying the programs we had there for the residents. My mother went to baseball games in Beloit and became a Beloit Brewers Mascot. She choked on some popcorn at a game and died. Mother was to be baptized the next day. I had prayed for years that she would accept Jesus as her Savior! Thank God she did! Then Ted died a month later from a heart attack. Ted was Catholic and received last rights.

A little lady was brought by her family to stay while they moved to New York. When they were settled, they planned to come back for her. She seemed confused and stopped eating well and was sad. Fred brought a baby goat to show the residents. She suddenly said, "Geise, Geise, Commen ze heren." She was German and didn't know our language! We had several staff members who spoke German. She brightened and ate well and related to all of us with interpreters until her family returned to take her to their new home. God was working again!

Rona Dolgner resigned and I became director of nurses. Then the facility was sold to people from Chicago. My problems began on the first day when the new owner visited. He pointed out things he would change then began to tell me about staff members that he wanted me to transfer to a different shift because he didn't like the way they looked and in one case he asked me to put something in the person's record and fire her because he didn't like her looks. This person was a little dwarf nurse's aide that we loved and who was excellent. I put her on the night shift and found transportation for her. I told him he wouldn't see her again. My conscience hurts that I didn't tell him that I didn't fire her but I was truthful that he would not see her during the day.

I made the changes that he suggested until he began to order things or procedures that were illegal in Wisconsin. He claimed they were okay in Illinois. I contacted Paul Ryan, and attorney in Janesville who gave me written statements supporting Wisconsin law to take to him. The owner was not happy but decided to accept the law. Then we had a court case in which we were at fault. The attorney told me to memorize the answer they wanted to the question that they had asked. I told the truth – they lost the case. In court, the attorney told the owner he had to get rid of "that one" he pointed to me. I was called into the office and was appointed assistant administrator which I wasn't qualified to be and I was given an office with no clear responsibilities. My assistant was promoted to director of nurses and she was not given an assistant.

We were due for a state inspection next month. They had bought only part of what they needed to keep the food the right temperature in the wings and refused to buy what they needed, so I bought the equipment and gave their book keeper the receipt because we had failed to pass the inspection before. We passed the inspection this time. The administrator demanded to see if they had been charged for the equipment that he had not authorized. I produced the receipt and told him why I bought it. I knew they were getting ready to fire me, so I got a position at Rock County Mental Hospital. Just as I prepared to give my two week notice I was called into the office and was told they couldn't afford an assistant administrator. They offered me a large amount of money to leave. I refused their offer and said I would take two week pay and leave that day. I left and was accepted as supervisor on the night shift at Rock County Mental Hospital.

Rock County Mental Hospital

About three months after I came, I received a call from the state nurse who conducted the state inspections of nursing homes. She told me that Caravilla had not passed inspection – that they had refused to comply, so they had been shut down. I received calls from some of the staff for job references that I supplied and they all found suitable jobs.

As a night supervisor I had three memorable experiences. First, there was a patient that lived on an Indian reservation and had no speech. I told him about my grandpa that was adopted by the Ogallala Sioux. He went around saying Ogallala Sioux and pointing to himself. I went too close to him when he was being held down one time and he kicked me. The next day he held his mouth and indicated he was sorry. I helped make arrangements for him to go to the Rock County Fair to see the Indian Dances. He was so happy. Second, an elderly woman put a doll in her bed and treated it like a baby. A new aide told her it was not a baby. Then she thought it died so she cried and wouldn't eat. I worked with staff and got permission to bury the baby. We had a funeral and then an aide gave her a new doll. She began to eat and enjoy life again. Third, I had a black aide who went to sleep on duty several times, which was dangerous for all of us. I finally disciplined her. I had a cold and she put a hex on me. I talked to her about what that meant and she told me she didn't go to church anymore. She told me she and others were going to a witch doctor from the islands. I knew her pastor and that she had been the church organist, so I called him. When he knew why she wasn't coming, he got together with the other black pastors and they won the people back to their congregations. She became the organist again and the pastor called me to tell me that she had taken communion and then died of a heart attack after playing the final hymn. God helped me find ways to meet these people's needs.

Foster Children

God prepared George and me to have foster children in many ways. George had been raised in a loving Christian family where he had learned responsibility as well as faith in Jesus Christ as his savior. He had an older brother and sister and two younger sisters. I had had a young brother to take care of, and many experiences similar to those which brought the foster children into our care – abuse from alcoholic parents who abandoned us, time spent in protective custody in jail, and frequent moves to live with different people. I also had come to faith in Jesus Christ as a young child and learned to trust Him to care for me.

Another experience that prepared us was that a stepfather brought his young son to work for us. He had been raised on a farm and thought the experience would be good for his son. Our children were small at that time and we needed his help, so he came to live with us. He was a good worker and got along well with our children. He told us that he had been abused by his stepfather and that his brother had been severely injured by him. His grandma was caring for the brother in Illinois. He had two sisters living at home that he called often and also visited his brother while he lived with us. He graduated from school and got a job as a salesman. Sadly, he was killed in an automobile accident just two years later.

One of my duties as a Public Health Nurse was to visit families that needed health services. On one visit, a young teenage boy asked me to talk to me privately in the back yard. He told me that he worked for Van Galder Bus Company cleaning out the school buses after school. He said that Mr. Van Galder had told him that I had a goat farm and that he could live with me as a foster child if I agreed. He said he wanted to finish high school but was having trouble because his mother and three younger sisters interfered so he couldn't do his homework. I said I didn't know about foster care. Then he pulled out papers from his pocket and said that he had gone to Social Services to get them. "You get paid for me and I get to work for you for free! But your husband has to agree." I told him I would ask him. He said he would work for Van Galder after school – then go home and see that his family was OK – then go to the farm with me. When I went to work he would return to his home and then go to school from there.

George agreed and so our work as foster parents began in 1966. Our oldest son, Fred, was 22 and was living at home with Martha who was 13. Tom and Linda were going to college in Iowa. I was a foster parent for the next forty-five years. George died in 1994 after several strokes, but I continued to care for one foster child until she was eighteen. She then decided to return from Arizona to Janesville to live with her family.

The purpose of my story is to show God working in my life and the lives of others I cared for. Because of privacy concerns, I cannot reveal the names of my foster children, but I will tell what I know of their stories that brought them to us.

Several of the boys had been beaten repeatedly, one girl had been locked in a basement for years, two girls had been raped, one girl had been abused by her mother, six girls were placed because of family problems. One girl had a mentally ill mother and when she was hospitalized, the daughter lived on the street and learned to defend herself and other skills necessary to survive in the winter. One of the boys was deaf and one girl was blind, two were mildly retarded. One boy had been placed in a holding cell in jail for protective custody until he could be placed in foster care.

God brought them to us so that they could be raised in a Christian home, go to Sunday school and church. They learned to help one another as well as to experience love and support as they grew up. We think of them as our own children and have maintained relationships with most of them until the present time. My foster family continues to grow as they have families of their own, now. Some have died and two that we had for a short time, we have lost contact with.

We took them on many trips to places in Wisconsin – The Dells, House on the Rock, Cave of the Mounds, Mt. Horeb, and Knott's Berry Farm. Some went to California, South Dakota, Canada, and Mexico with us to experience the wonderful world we live in.

We had to learn how to help them learn to forgive their parents and others that abused them. They had problems at school with mistreatment and needed help to make friends and learn their lessons. We had to learn how to help the blind girl and the deaf boy to relate to us and each other. God helped us, too!

Family Trips

Family trips were an important part of our family life. Because George and I were so busy with our jobs, community work, and the goat dairy, we were not able to spend much quality time with our children as we needed to develop the bonds of love that we all need. Through trips together we were able to share our wonder at the awesome world God had placed us in and see His hand in all our experiences there and in the lives of the people we loved.

There were many short trips in Wisconsin, longer trips in the United States, one to Alaska, two to Hawaii, two to Canada and one to Europe where we visited Holland, Germany, Luxembourg, and Switzerland. Because my emphasis in this story is my journey with God, many trips and details will be omitted.

The first trips George and I took were with our four children to explore many points of interest in our state of Wisconsin: the Dells, Cave of the Mounds, fairs, pageants, circuses, factories, dairies, an emu farm and a strawberry farm. About once a year after about 1958, we traveled back east to Maryland, Virginia, Washington, DC and Pennsylvania to visit relatives. We went to Chicago to see a museum and a film on the Star that the wise men followed to Bethlehem.

On one of our visits to see my father in Washington, DC, in a diner that served as the office of the cab company my father worked for, George, Tom, Linda and I had an interesting experience. A limousine drove up and a man walked in and sat down with us. The people at the diner became quiet until we started to talk. After a little while the man looked at his watch and said he had to go to work. Tom asked him what kind of work he did. It got quiet again. The man got nervous, then he smiled and said he was an insurance agent and laughed. The people started talking again and he was driven off. After we left the diner, my father told us the man was a drug dealer and visited the apartment buildings that surrounded us. We saw Satan at work!

I will add one more note here… My father was an alcoholic who went for treatment many times. I prayed for him, he knew. One morning when he was in his sixties, he called me and told me he

My Journey with God • 179

had gone to church and taken communion that morning. He said he had been free of alcohol for a year that day because he had found a pastor who helped him every day. He died a month later.

While we were in Virginia, we saw God working in the life of George's sister, Ruth. She was transformed from a self-centered controlling capable young woman to a bedridden Christ-centered loving woman who was devoting her life to helping people to have transportation to church, doctors and to meet other needs. She also reconnected to her family. She did all this through her phone! She died young from complications of diabetes, which she had had since childhood. When we were in Maryland we visited my Uncle Harwood, whose hired man had been killed by a sow while he was working for him. He was caring for his hired man's family as his own, sending his children to college with his own. My Aunt Verdie was being cared for by a neighbor who loved her. George asked him why he cared for her and his reply was "Why not?"

George planned a car trip for the children and me to Yellowstone Park. Tom had his license, so he shared some of the driving responsibilities with me. He became ill, so we stopped in Salt Lake City to see a doctor. He treated Tom and made arrangements for us to stay at a motel for two days if we promised to visit the Mormon Temple and see all the exhibits. We kept our promise. He made arrangements for one more doctor visit along our way to Wyoming!

In Yellowstone it was awesome to see the eruption of the geyser and realize that all that fire and steam is under our feet. On a trail ride, Fred's horse got spooked and took off running across a meadow. The leader raced to catch up to them, then calmed the horse down. He also reassured Fred before returning them to the line of horses. We saw a man trying to film a herd of buffalo in a field. The herd began to move the calves and cows into the middle, then the bulls put their tails up and heads down, and charged! The man lost his camera, but made it under the fence in time! God taught the bulls how to protect their calves and cows! We enjoyed seeing so much beauty in God's creations.

We saw the other side of nature, too. A bear ran past me to a garbage can by the road, sat down, and proceeded to eat the garbage! I was locked out of the combi at the time because the children were afraid of the bear. Going out of the park, there had been a small earthquake that destroyed part of the road. We couldn't move as we were bumper to bumper. One car had gone over the cliff and landed on a ledge below. Rescuers were going down to help them. Finally, we began to go forward. Workers offered to drive, but I chose to do it myself. It was rough, but we were together and made it. We were praying hard!

On our way to the east coast early one Sunday morning we stopped at a little church in the hill country. The pastor told me the service would be longer than usual because it would be a reconciliation service between two Indian clans that had been feuding for many years. He had had to have two services for all the ten years he had been there until this Sunday. The service opened with prayers and then the pastor preached on Jesus' answer to the questions of obtaining salvation in Luke 10:29-33 then on forgiveness in Matthew 6:14. Then members took turns standing, stating what they had done to others, asking for forgiveness, and receiving it. Others stood and accused others and pardoned them. This went on for about an hour. Then a man and woman came forward with pitch pipes and led the congregation in hymns. The pastor concluded the service with the Lord's Prayer and they were dismissed for the potluck dinner. I have cherished the memory ever since!

George and I took a trip to San Francisco with Grandma Reuss to see her sister that she had not seen since she was married. They talked and drank coffee all night! They wanted to see each other, so George and I decided to go to a national park and then to see Grandma Peggy. We would come back for Grandma Reuss. In the park we went up on one mountain to see a waterfall on another mountain. While we were enjoying the view, George said it was getting dark. His lips were blue! I agreed, put my arm around him and barely made it back to the car to put him in! When we got back down, he woke up! I had forgotten about the hole in his heart! We saw a hammock hanging from the middle of a high cliff. We were told a person would sleep there and then continue to climb to the top the next day!

We picked Grandma Reuss up and took her to El Paso. There were no alligators in the park by the hotel then. We went to Juarez to sight see. Grandma made friends with a man there who was a guide. He took us to his home for lunch and helped us go across the border and gave us gifts! He and Grandma continued to write each other until Grandma died!

I made two trips to Hawaii. The first trip was with Fred. He had won two days and nights over the phone. I don't know the details. We stayed in a hotel which was close to a tourist center. There we met a handicapped lady from Janesville who was a clerk there! She begged us not to tell anyone where she was because her family did not want her to have a job. She would write a letter for us to mail when we got back to Chicago. She said she tried to write to them every month and have the letters mailed from many places. She wanted to visit one of the islands, but needed to have help to get on the small plane, so we helped her and got a free tour of that island also!

We took a tour of Hawaii that was part of our winning. The volcano and the lava were there to remind us that this is the center of our planet that God made. The tropical fruits: mangoes, pineapples, coconuts reminders of the variety of foods He made to nourish us. Pearl Harbor reminded us of the horrors of war. We saw other wonders of the sea through glass bottomed boats and clothes made of plants and experienced the friendship of the Hawaiian people.

Foster children and I took a train trip to see Grandma Peggy in Los Angeles. Riding in the observation seats on the roof was very interesting. She had a pet monkey that jumped on shoulders and bit our ears. The house was covered with monkey pee. The window glass was covered so we couldn't see out. We stayed in a tent in the backyard, but we enjoyed visiting with Ted and Grandma. We went to Disneyland but it was Gay Day. I told the children everyone was wearing a costume.

After George's stroke, Linda and Doug took us to Germany to see Marty who was going to a university in Freiberg as an exchange student. George needed a wheelchair and had limited use of his right arm, but was otherwise in good health.

We flew with Linda and Doug to Amsterdam, Holland, where we stayed in an upstairs rooming house. An interesting story here. When we arrived, I asked the landlady for directions to the bathroom. She told me to wait a minute. It was longer than a minute. Then she took me down the hall and opened the door. She saw my surprised face, so she said "Oh, you want the vaser closet!" In the middle of the room was a bathtub on a wooden platform with a gas fire burning under it! There were steps up to the tub, so I looked in to see a wooden plank on the bottom. She told me that if I was in England I should ask for the loo. I had to pay for the bath.

We visited the apartment that Anne Frank had lived in and several other attractions that reminded us of the Holocaust. We saw auctions of flowers and cheeses that were flown all over Europe. There was a museum where we saw students on the floor sketching some of the masterpieces that were the result of God's gift to men. The windmills and canals reminded me of the little book my great grandpa had given me, "The Little Dutch Twins."

Linda and Doug took us to Germany then to visit Martha. She had lived upstairs from a bakery, but her landlord had died, so she had to move into the university dorm. We met her in town after we were settled in our bed and breakfast. We visited many attractions with her. One street dance was interesting. Except for the wooden shoes and the step-hop, it reminded me of our square dance. Linda and Doug left us to travel to other countries. They made arrangements to meet us in Switzerland. We saw Bob Ames from Janesville. He was stationed at an army base there.

Martha made arrangements for us to take a tour on the Rhine River. She was taking a final exam so she would have to meet us at the dock. The boat was revving up to move out when we heard, "Olympic! Olympic!" yells. There was Martha running at full tilt to catch the tour. The sailors flipped her on board. The captain scolded them.

We went to see a cathedral that had a room to torture people during the inquisition. The churches were built by people who were earning their way to heaven as they were promised we were told. No wonder there was a reformation!

I needed a blue rain hat for George, as it had started to rain when we were getting ready to leave, so I went into a hat store. The lady asked me if I spoke German and I said "No," so she left. I thought about each word, so when she came back with a man, I said, "Blau regen hut" and the man went out and slammed the door. I got her in trouble! I told her I was sorry in English. I think she understood that I only spoke baby German. George said how glad he was to see the country where his mother had lived.

We went to Luxembourg next on a train. It was afternoon, and I needed to put George to bed for a nap in the hotel because he was so tired. I wanted to plan a trip for us to a museum and to see an old Roman road the next day, so I went across the plaza in front of the hotel to a bus station in front of the train station. I heard a man calling for help and saw him lying under the bus behind the front wheels! People were paying him no attention as they got on the bus! I called to a tall black man who was selling something and he came, jumped in front of the bus that had started to rev its motor, got the man up on his crutches, took him to a taxi stand, paid his fare, and waved goodbye! I saw the Good Samaritan in action!

I decided that a cab was a better choice for George, so I climbed in. The driver asked if I spoke French and I said no. From that time on he smiled at me and spoke very complimentary things in English, but insulted me in French while he ran my bill up. When we got to the museum, he took my money, turned around and drove off after yelling, "Ferme!" The museum was closed. It was a religious holiday! I climbed up to the top of the hill to look down to find our hotel which was by a river. Then I walked back. It seemed to be a long way. I went into a Cathedral to sit down. It had been bombed during the war and one section was new and it blended perfectly with the ancient side. Then there was another long walk to the hotel.

We went to supper in a formal dining room and had a fabulous supper. There was a note on the table saying not to give tips, so we didn't. Serious mistake! The next morning when we went to breakfast we were not served. I went to the hotel manager who checked with the dining room and said we had insulted the dining room staff by not tipping. There was nothing he could do. I offered to pay. It was refused. I went out into the plaza and brought in our breakfast and ate it in the dining room.

We decided to go to Switzerland then and the manager did help me make arrangements. The bell boy was the son of the chef, so he would not help us. When we came out, the plaza was full of cars, the policeman was blowing his whistle and no one seemed to pay attention. I saw some boys playing on the sidewalk and asked them if they spoke English. They said yes, but you speak American! They formed a wedge and got us across to the train station, down the freight elevator, and onto the train. One boy got my ticket paid. They wouldn't take any money – said it was fun! I really learned what it feels like to be discriminated against, and also God helped me out of a bad situation.

We met Linda and Doug in Switzerland and were treated well there. It was awesome to see the Alps, lakes and rivers. I had to watch George as we went over the mountains in a train that was pulled over the peak by cables! We rode in a ship on lake with a wedding party that left us in a beautiful horse drawn carriage. We met a nurse in her nineties who visited her clients on foot every day. We saw a cemetery where bodies were being exhumed and taken to a crypt because of the scarcity of land for burials. What a fabulous trip!

I made five trips to Mexico and I have already told you about the first trip with George when we were threatened, so I will include one more that is interesting to me. George and I went with two foster girls. We stayed with a school friend of Linda's. She was now a licensed tour guide in Mexico and taught English to businessmen who wanted to learn English.

We then went to Mexico City to museums there. Between one foster child who had taken Spanish in school, and I, who had five years of Latin, we translated all the written material because we couldn't understand the museum tour guide's English. God had prepared us! We went to an unusual restaurant called *Restaurante Comerciale*. The tables where we were to eat were in little cubicles. Each was a different business setting, but ours was a jail cell! We were served through a large door that was barred. The staff put on musical stage shows every half hour and the food was *deliciosa*!

We went to a high school graduation for the daughter of our local hosts the last day we were there. It started at 10 AM and lasted until 4 PM, with a buffet at noon. 9th, 10th, and 11th graders each put on a stage play, after which the formal graduation took place! That night after dinner, our host sang for us. He was an opera star! What a marvelous visit!

With foster children and Grandsons Jon and Pete, we celebrated the national bicentennial by taking a train to Jamestown, then Washington, DC, and finally Philadelphia. It was very interesting to see the exhibits, but sad to see the large crowds being made dangerous by people slashing purses in Philadelphia.

Linda and Doug took us on our second trip to Hawaii. Doug's mother, Loris, went with us. She was a reporter for the local newspaper and interviewed the pilot who took us over the volcano and other persons of interest to her. We took tours, saw dances and thoroughly enjoyed our visit. George had been stationed there during the war and he said he saw some changes. He had not seen the black sand beach or the dancing natives before.

We took a trip with all of our children, their spouses and our grandchildren on the Mississippi River to go through the locks. It was so interesting to see how locks could connect rivers, lakes and oceans.

Linda and Martha took me to visit most of the places I had lived as a child. What a wonderful adventure! The house where I had lived in York was the same and the drug store had been enlarged. The house I lived in in Hagerstown was an apartment house now. The Episcopal Church had no doors on the pews, but the beautiful brass depiction of Jesus' life was still on the wall behind the altar. There was a picture on the wall of the pastor with a full white beard.

As we traveled, most of the things were the same, but I needed directions to the house in Elizabethtown where I had lived with Grandma and Grandpa Lee, so I asked a man walking his dog. He told me and then exclaimed, "I know you! You are the patrol girl who sent the lady who was bothering me to help the lost children in the Masonic Temple in the flood in Harrisburg. I was working on the bridge!" How about that for a coincidence!

We visited a cousin in Virginia that told me about his deliverance from his addiction to alcohol. His wife had said she would give him one more chance to go to a counselor. He had tried treatment before without success. Now he was debating as to whether to go or not as he drove home to meet her. Suddenly as he turned into his driveway, he saw a rainbow that he had to drive through to reach his wife as she waited for him! He knew it was God that sent it to him to choose to go to the therapist! He went and is successful to this day in Alcoholics Anonymous.

Marty and Tom took me to Alaska with their children. We went on a tour and saw what was left after the severe earthquake of 1964. They showed us a fabulous video of the northern lights; they were beautiful! I had seen them before, one night in Janesville and got the family up to see them.

We took a tour on a bus through Denali National Park. Tourists were not allowed to hike in the park unless they had passed a test given after they had been instructed by staff and had the right equipment. We saw over a hundred animals in their native environment – we kept notes! I marveled at the coordination of the eagles and bears as they caught salmon as they jumped their way upstream to spawn.

After the bus tour, we watched whales circling around a school of fish in a bay, then suddenly diving and coming up with mouths full of fish! In a bay, I saw an otter floating on its back with an oyster in its shell on its chest. He had a stone to crush the shell and was eating the meat. Then I had an adventure!

The grandchildren had gone to explore a fort on the bay and Marty and Tom took a boat tour to see the glaciers, so I took a little map that the office had given me and started to hike in the woods by myself. I followed the axe marks on the trees until I was about half way, when I heard the birds and squirrels making a lot of noise. I stopped and stared at a wolf! He stared at me! It seemed like forever and I said a prayer. Then he turned and walked away! I looked at my map and decided to keep going forward as it was a shorter way home. I met a handicapped man in a wheelchair with a big husky dog walking beside him, He asked what made the noise and said, "You were lucky! If it had been a bear, you would have been dead." He carried a rifle. I didn't tell the family until we were going home. Of course they scolded me!

The trips showed me how important it was that I had had the experiences I had as a child. By being neglected, hungry, frightened and abused, I lived to appreciate the loving concern God showed me by the many people He sent to nurture and guide me. I also learned how to forgive those who neglected or abused me. Most of all, it reinforced my love for God and the need to show it by loving others.

I will continue, now, by picking up the story of my career chronology.

Skaalen Home

At Skaalen Home, I worked the night shift for the nursing home unit. It was on the 5th floor of a complex which also included independent and assisted living facilities. I was the charge nurse, giving medications and treatments, as well as securing blood for the lab ordered for the morning. I was responsible for first aid and also responsible for the assisted living area at night. I had several nursing assistants working with me.

I had one experience there which I want to include in this. I have no memory of this incident, but many years later I returned to Skaalen Home to volunteer. As I was walking down the hall, a tall black nurse came behind me and hugged me. I was surprised. "You don't remember me, do you?" she said. I told her "No." Then she told me this story.

> She had been a resident assistant. It was her first day on the job. She had made a mistake and had hidden in a closet to cry, since she was sure she would be fired. I found her, got down on my knees, and coaxed her out of the closet. I held her in my arms as she confessed what she had done. She told me I told her we all make mistakes, including me. She then told me to wash my face and hands, and that we must fix the problem, that she would not be fired. She said that she was so relieved she decided then and there that she would study to be a nurse like me. She also said that I was the first white person to ever touch her.

I included this story because it shows how simple acts of kindness can influence others, even when we are not aware of it. We affect others when we act, especially when we act as Jesus wants us to.

The other story I want to include is very different... Every morning I drove back to my home in Janesville on a back-country road. One day a hawk flew low, in front of the car for two crossroads (two mile). Then it landed on a branch of the tree at the crossroad.

Every morning, it repeated this the whole time I worked there! I came to look for it and feel God's presence!

George loved being in Skaalen. He sang in the choir and did some work in the workshop with help. He received the care he needed much better than at home. Because he made friends there and enjoyed the programs and church services, we decided it was best to keep him there.

Leaving Janesville

I decided to sell the farm and had taken in a homeless man to help with the move. At that point, I only had Fred and one foster child to care for. I had a chance to work closer to home at Cedar Crest, a nursing home in Janesville, so I took a position as a night nurse there. I visited George twice a week as well as daily phone calls.

At that point, his cancer began spreading very rapidly in his lymph system. One night we were eating supper when he said he was not hungry and wanted to go to bed. He asked to kiss me goodbye at his bedside, so we managed to stand and embrace. The next morning, the nurse called and told me that he had died. He had asked for a pain pill for the first time, and when she brought it to his room she found that he had passed away. It was just the way he hoped to die. That was in November 1994. He was cremated and his ashes were placed on our farm as he had requested.

At Cedar Crest, I was able to provide care to Mr. Meton, the man who had taught Fred how to care for bees. He said Fred was the only person he had ever know who could handle the bees without ever being stung. I will tell about this in the chapter on family. I also cared for some of our former neighbors, the Austins. I also became friends with a nurse there, June Loercher, who I still communicate with.

When the farm was sold, I decided to move to Stoughton to be near my daughter, Martha, and her husband, Tom. I still travelled back and forth to work at Cedar Crest until one night when I was blown into another lane by a huge truck as I was on my way to work. It was very icy and I nearly crashed into another car. I decided then that I would resign from Cedar Crest and reapply at Skaalen to work closer to home.

When I applied, I was told that there was no opening for a nurse but there was a nurses assistant position available. This was a position that allowed the individual to pass medications and do treatments, but did not require assessment of the patient's needs or conditions. The latter had to be done by a registered nurse. I asked if I could apply and the Director of Nurses hesitated. Suddenly I knew her problem. She could not discriminate against me because of my age, but some of the patient care was possibly more physical than I was capable of at 80. I asked her to tell the person in charge of the Skaalen Home gym program what I had to do and when I could do it to tell her and then I could apply. I got the job! I worked there until I moved to Arizona when I was 82. It was the last job I had as a nurse, although I've been using all the skills I was given by God for all the years since.

While I was in Stoughton a tornado touched down. The roof of the house across the street blew off and there was a lot of damage to the farms north of us. A farmer told this story. He was walking (very discouraged) down the path where his barn had been, when he saw a strange man with a black hat and beard walking towards him with outstretched arms. He walked right into them and felt a warm hug. All his anxiety went away as the man said, "God loves you. He will be with you through this! Peace be with you." It was an Amish man who had come from Pennsylvania with friends to help rebuild the devastated farms. They did just that! The next year a tornado struck Pennsylvania and the farmers from Stoughton helped them. What a witness for Jesus!

Arizona

I moved into an apartment in Chandler Arizona with Fred and my last foster child. She was in high school and Doug helped me make arrangements for her to enter a private school. I volunteered to help children there with English as they were referred to me. This was very interesting, and I did this one morning each week all the time we were there.

We went to Gethsemane Lutheran Church there. I volunteered each week to work with a group there that was writing 1st Corinthians in Braille for the blind. I checked each book when it was finished to be sure it was correct. Fred also helped prepare the books for mailing. My hearing had begun to fail, and I had a hearing aid, but still had trouble hearing what the group was laughing about when they were talking. I explained that I often heard them incorrectly. They were patient with me after that. This remains a problem for me to this day.

The church also had a prison ministry through their church in Phoenix. I wrote letters to prisoners in the prison that had been referred to our church and they responded by writing to me at my church address. I had eight prisoners when I left, and referred all but one to other church members. That one the others did not want was a Jew who had been converted, so I got permission to give him my address in Wisconsin when I moved there.

The eighth prisoner and I had a very good relationship. He did not return my letters once for six weeks. When the correspondence resumed, he said he had told some new prisoners that they needed to repent or go to hell when they died. They beat him, broke his nose gave him a concussion and a broken hip and shoulder in reply. I wrote him and told him the first message must be love. He said he took my letter to the pastor and he said I was right! He said he was transferred to a unit named "Meadows" and that he was no longer in a cell. He did not like to be in a dormitory – he was afraid. I asked him who was there and he said that there were blind, old and handicapped people there. He came to really enjoy the freedom and said he has helped to convert some men there.

I have a cross that a prisoner made of white string. It has a heart with a tiny cross in the middle. Another prisoner made me a black cross of nails on a black string. I also have a jewelry box made of tiny paper rolls that look like wood. One of the prisoners was moved to other prisons to teach them how to do this. I came to appreciate their letters as we shared our faith.

I also worked at St. Vincent DePaul in Phoenix on some Saturdays with my daughter's church, the Phoenix Church of Christ. We served the noon meal to homeless people. What an experience! I worked with the people who did not have children and were not handicapped except that there were many mentally ill people. These people were treated if they harmed others or themselves, then they were put back on the street. I saw some people feeding others who they had brought in with them. I referred them right away to the staff who cared for them. There was another section for women with children and handicapped people.

While we were there, my foster child often went to the city park which was right beside our apartment with her friends. One day they came running back, laughing, out of breath. She said that they had been walking along the path when a man grabbed her cell phone out of her hand and ran off. They ran after him and reached him as a car pulled up and opened the door. She grabbed the phone out of his hand and they ran back to our apartment! I took them to the police station in the park where the officer told her that many girls had been kidnapped and taken to Mexico there. He was surprised that more men had not jumped out to capture them. Then one of the girls said she did look back and saw two more, but they zigzagged around trees until they were among people, so they didn't follow. From that time on, I went to the park with them.

Fred got a job at Fry's grocery store, working in the parking lot and cleaning in the store. He noticed a fellow employee swaying in the bathroom and prevented him from hitting his head as he fell unconscious to the floor. He had told Fred that if anything happened to him that his on doctor had to be called. His number was around his neck on a necklace. Fred called the number, then ran to tell the manager. Because he did this, the management gave him a picnic and an award. He also gave suggestions for improvement to the management and received "Employee of The Year" awards every year he was there.

I taught teenagers in Sunday School at Church. I had them bring articles from newspapers and magazines or tell of experiences they had that made the bible lessons pertinent for them.

Linda's mother-in-law received poor care in the hospital there, so went to a nursing home where she received good care until she died. One day when my foster child and I were visiting her, she looked up and spoke to a vision of her daughter who had died. This was a wonderful experience for all of us!

For the first time I was able to enjoy a relationship with my granddaughter Rachel and her family – husband Brandon, son Noah and daughter Taryn. I was so busy with my family, volunteering and spending some time in the pool near our apartment that I did not make friends for myself.

One Friday evening, I bent over to kiss my foster daughter good night, I hit my big toe on the leg of a small table and dislocated it. Doug took me to the hospital emergency room, where I spent five hours, but was not treated because the doctor didn't know how to relocate it! I was kept in the hospital until Monday after finally having it relocated! It took five hours for the doctor that signed the final release for all the patients to come!

The reason I included this story is that I got bed bugs in the waiting room! The hospital told me when I traced the infestation! I was originally misdiagnosed because my bites caused large swellings on my body. This went on for weeks as I was referred to several doctors and was scheduled to go to a cancer hospital on Monday. The Friday before my appointment, at around midnight my foster daughter found a little brown bug on her leg that bit her. She went to Fred's room and found him watching a TV program on bed bugs!. They went to her bed and found many under the mattress cover and many more under Fred's. They woke me and I had the most!! Fred and she had had bites, too but we had mosquitoes, so we all thought they were mosquito bites.

Of course the management was notified and an extermination business was called. After three treatments it was decided that we had to move. Two neighboring apartments had been infested through the electric fixtures in the wall. Most of my furniture went to the dump. I laughed because we had gotten our furniture at the dump in Indiana once when we had moved from the trailer! What goes around comes around!

We made arrangements to move to Wisconsin then as it would be hard to rent again there. We also had to take our foster daughter home to Wisconsin as she had turned eighteen. My other daughter was there as well as former foster children. God was working in our lives in strange and wonderful ways again!

Stoughton

We lived with Martha at first because the apartment complex needed to prepare an apartment for us. It was a HUD complex which was run by the government. Fred had an apartment in a different building from me because his income was lower. After trying to get a job on his own, he contacted a government office in Madison that dealt with persons who had development disabilities. They provided a worker who came to Stoughton to help him. They were not successful.

We attended Good Shepherd By The Lake Lutheran Church. They had a ministry in Madison volunteering service at Bethesda Thrift Store. This store's income supported two homes for handicapped people. Our church provided about ten people once a month for a day plus one more day if there were five weeks. Fred and I volunteered about a month after we moved to Stoughton.

He worked in donations like he had done in Goodwill in Janesville. After several years, the manager offered him a job Monday, Wednesday and Friday from 10 am until 3:30 pm. I continued to volunteer on those days. We thoroughly enjoyed the fellowship there. Fred drove and the manager arranged different hours and days if the weather was bad. Fred was treated very well and I had a chance to help organize the work I was doing to be more productive and comfortable for the handicapped people I worked with. We worked there until two days before he had a stroke on my 92nd birthday.

During that time, we volunteered at Skaalen Home on Tuesdays and the Senior Center and Nazareth Home on Thursdays. At the nursing homes, we visited with residents who were assigned to us and others that we came to know from the community. I also visited with people in the Alzheimer's unit at Skaalen Home and Fred played cribbage with residents there. At Nazareth, he played other card games with a group of residents.

We were able to minister to these people. In one case, I helped a lady to find a pastor to baptize her before she died. In another case we helped a man who had asked for us because he was so angry at the way God had treated him. Most of the time, we visited people who were lonely. Both of us felt that we were doing what God wanted us to do. I also found a pastor whose mission was to visit nursing homes, to meet the needs of two of the men we served when we left to go back to Arizona five years later. At the Senior Center, we cleaned the equipment that was donated and helped to serve lunch and do the dishes.

We attended church regularly. Martha was a Sunday school teacher and the choir director. We heard wonderful music. One black lady sang a spiritual I had not heard since I was a child. I found my eyes tearing. They provided a special bulletin for handicapped people that Fred appreciated very much. Everyone was very nice to Fred. The church had programs for summer school for community children in a park that I helped with, and had other programs to help a school in town that had poor people. I had been wanting to be baptized by immersion and the pastor did this for me in the pool at Skaalen Home. I appreciated that very much. The sermons were excellent and we enjoyed the fellowship.

At the apartment, we made friends with other residents. Two men resented Fred's coming to my apartment, but I confronted both of them and was finally able to get them to accept him by explaining Fred's handicap and helping them get needed clothing at the thrift store. They were not accepted by the other residents because of their behavior. There was a lady across the hall from me that was from Mexico and did not understand English very well, so she did not come to gathering in the dining room. Just for special occasions when several of us invited her and helped her participate. She really enjoyed that. She was interested in my mission in South America with Child International and began to write to the child I was sponsoring in Spanish. She continued until she died.

During the whole time we were in Stoughton, we enjoyed fellowship with Martha and Tom, other people we met at church, and renewed relationship with former foster children and their families. It was so interesting to see God working in everyone's lives! I will now talk about how He worked in ours to bring us back to Arizona and to our present residence.

Return to Arizona

Fred and I had just signed the paperwork to share an apartment in Stoughton when he had a stroke in late 2015. We lived together there as he recovered, but decided to move back to Arizona in 2016. We moved to Brookdale North Chandler, a facility that provides independent and assisted living as well as skilled nursing care.

Fred's last stroke affected his speech the most. At first, he could only speak one or two words. Now, three years later, with effort about what he is thinking he can say a sentence in a high-pitched voice. However, he can sing hymns in his normal voice. He said he memorized them long ago because he could not read fast enough! He can still play cribbage, Rummicube, and bingo. He is in good health, takes medicine for his heart, and uses a walker. He takes care of himself except he has help with bathing three times a week. He goes to adult three times a week for programs for exercise.

At 96, I enjoy good health and use a walker also. I take care of myself and participate in games, exercise programs and programs that improve my mind. I help make mats for homeless, and participate in other programs to help others when they are offered. I am ambassador in my ba for the residents on first floor. I welcome new residents and help them adjust to the program the facility offers. I keep them updated weekly on the programs the facility offers.

Fred and I attend church regularly on Sunday (Linda and Doug take us) and attend other programs the church offers. We have Bible study, games and prayers together every night. I am so thankful we can be together!

My Husband

I decided to put my husband's story here for his family. George Reuss is an essential part of my life and theirs. I will write what I remember about his life before I met him and add some things I did not cover in my story so far.

He had a beautiful singing voice until his voice changed. His father was the church organist and his mother sang in the choir. People who heard him sing "O Holy Night" at the Christmas service said it was the most beautiful they had ever heard.

His best friend was the next-door neighbor, Harry. He loved to play baseball and rode a bike.

He went to the University of Virginia in Charlottesville and graduated from there with a BA in electrical engineering. While there, he worked for the pastor in the fall and winter, painting his home and doing odd jobs for the congregation. He told me he worked in the circus one summer. He walked a tightrope with a balance pole while twirling something in his mouth. I have a picture that he gave me of this. He also swallowed a sword! He said he couldn't taste anything for a week afterward, but it paid good money!

He came to visit me in Niagara Falls one summer and took me to meet his grandparents on his father's side. They were from Berlin and told me that his mother's family did not speak proper German. They were Lutherans as were his mother's family. We played tennis while he visited and he fell and was unconscious for a short time. He told my grandfather and me that he was born with a hole in his heart and was not supposed to exercise too much.

When I visited him at the university, he arranged for me to dance with other men except for the first and last dances. He walked me around the floor the, he never learned to dance, and didn't want me to after we were married. He gave me permission at Tom's wedding. He said that he also worked on the Muncaster's farm one summer. That is where I met him because I was working there, too, for my cousin Eleanor's husband John.

After he graduated, he went to work for the Power and Light Company in Alexandria, Virginia until the war came. He entered the service in the Army Air Force and eventually became a Lieutenant. He was sent to El Paso, Texas, where we were married in 1943. I met Bill and Vivian Roine at the wedding. They remained friends from then on. Bill was in the army with George throughout the war. After the wedding, we rented an apartment in El Paso for a short time. Then George was sent to Florida for additional training. On return, George was sent to an air base in Clarkesville, Tennessee.

While we were living in the home of the Runyans, I became very ill due to my pregnancy. George was able to be there when Fred was born. Subsequently, he went to Saipan, Tinian, and finally, to Okinawa. He was there when the atomic bomb was dropped and flew home the day after to Hawaii, then to Washington, DC, then to Richmond. His father had had a stroke and the war department allowed him to return home because he was ill, too, with the flu.

After he came back from the service, we lived in a little town outside of Richmond with Fred. The baby became very sick with encephalitis and the doctor said he would be severely brain damaged and should be put in an institution. George signed the papers, but I would not, so he said "He's your baby, then." And he was.

When we were having dinner at his parents' house, an army officer came looking for George. He was invited to dinner and proceeded to tell us that George was to receive a special award for bravery in the war. George got up and asked the man to step into the hall with him. Soon we heard the door shut and the man was gone. George came back to the table and said he had done nothing anyone else would not have done. He would never discuss it again.

We took trips with the children when they were growing up to see family back east. George planned them and drove. We thoroughly enjoyed them. He loved to travel!

We had taken in a boy to help with the dairy in the 1950's. After we built the new house and Linda was in college, we took in foster children, mostly girls. In all, we had 22 foster children, only three boys. George was very good with them and enjoyed them all. He was active in the development of the sheltered workshop and supportive of me with the many projects I was involved in in public health. He helped with bowling for handicapped that now is Special Olympics. He was on the Janesville City School board for two terms.

We attended St. Paul's Lutheran Church for many years. Then I was excommunicated by the pastor because I held a patient's hands while the priest was giving last rites. He said it was participating in a heathen rite. I said it was Christian and I would need to do it again if necessary as I was a nurse. George said we must leave and go to Faith Lutheran Church. It was ELCA where his brother directed him to go. He found out that I was not officially excommunicated as it did not go to the bishop. George was active in Faith Lutheran Church and I taught Sunday school. He was Sunday School Principal for a while before we left because of the abortion issue. We went to New Hope Lutheran Church, a TALC denomination. Then we came back to St. Paul's when that church closed and St. Paul's had a new pastor.

After the goat dairy was shut down George, continued to use his engineering and mechanical skills to earn money. He worked for Gilman Engineering. He had inventions there I know. He worked for Fairbanks Morse in Beloit for many years later.

He worked at Warner Brake Corp, too. There, he invented a machine that was patented and the company altered the design when he told them not to. He warned them that it would not do what they sold it for and offered to redesign it, but they refused so he left. The altered design caused some deaths and property damage that the company tried to sue him for. The patent office defended him successfully. George thanked God for His help with the patent office.

He worked at car dealers, I think, before his last stroke. Maybe Tom remembers. He was very versatile in his jobs, using skills God gave him. George had several heart attacks before he had his strokes.

In around 1971, George was in the hospital after a heart attack and was to come home the next day. He was left alone from 9 AM until Fred and I came at 5 PM. Fred found him in a room where the floor was being refinished, behind a screen in a regular chair with his right leg black. I made them call his doctor from home. They put him to bed with a hot pack for his leg and under a metal cradle. The next day, an aide took it all off as she had been accustomed to do, and put him through range of motion. This sent the clots through his body. He was unconscious for three days.

When Fred and I came that evening the nurse told us he was dead – that the cart to take him to the morgue was in the hall. We could see him as he had died while we were on our way. When I saw him, I put my head on his chest and heard a heartbeat! Fred put the oxygen mask on and I persuaded the nurse to listen, too. She called the doctor, who stamped down the hall and listened. He looked at the nurse and said, "What will we do with the paper work?"

The next day I told the administrator that George did not believe in suits, but I wanted a nurse around the clock until he died or was discharged. I said the insurance company would not pay, but they agreed to placing the extra watch. He went to Veteran's hospital when he recovered enough and then home. He lived at home from then on. He could not use his left arm but could talk and walk and enjoy life.

We had trips that our children took us on to their homes, up the Mississippi river, to Europe, and to Hawaii. He thoroughly enjoyed them all. George eventually needed around the clock care because he developed lymphatic cancer and it became harder for him to walk. I was not able to care for him as easily because of a fall.

We found a place for him in the nursing home section at Rock County. I saw him for breakfast and supper but he kept saying, "No food, no food." Then I checked his weight and he lost quite a few pounds. I checked with the kitchen and he hadn't eaten the noon meal for a month. He had an ulcer on his foot that was treated in the morning then he was wheeled to the nurse's station at noon where he missed his noon meal. I told the charge nurse and she said, "What do you expect me to do about it?"

I had him transferred to Skaalen Home in Stoughton where I represented Faith Lutheran church on their board. He enjoyed Skaalen Home where he sang in the choir and worked in woodworking. His lymphatic cancer suddenly grew into all his glands, but he was only uncomfortable enough to ask for medicine the night he died quietly in his sleep in 1994.

I could see God working in his life as I wrote what I remembered of his life and you can probably see more than I. He had experience with God in Sunday school and church from infancy and had practicing Christian parents to nurture his faith. He worked with chickens at first, then animals on the farm to prepare him for the goat dairy. He got a good education, both in school, then in vocational school and college. God gifted him in math. He learned to use his skills in the jobs he held and had experience in life in the service. He learned to work for others in developing the engineering program in college and in working with others on the farm and in his jobs. He refused to alter his design when he knew it would harm others and left his job as the price. He was a good father as God wanted him to be to foster children, too. He learned to control his temper. He was able to help handicapped people and others that God put in his life. These are just a few examples that I see. There are more!

My Children

I must now include the most important part of my journey with God – my children.

I have written about Fred's birth, but I didn't tell about his homecoming. Aunt Jinny and Bobby (age 5) met me at the door. "Put him down so I can play with him!" exclaimed Bobby.

"No, he's too little to play with you now." I said.

Then he asked if he could hear him and see him. I told him that he probably could do both, but he could not talk to him yet. Then Aunt Jinny took him upstairs for his nap. I took him to our apartment in Aunt Jinny's house to get him settled in his crib and we visited with Grandma and Aunt Jinny until it was time to get Bobby up from his nap. He was nowhere to be found!

Finally, we called the police. Then we got a phone call from a nurse at the hospital about ten blocks away across streets and a busy highway. "We have a little boy here who remembered his phone number. He told us that he came to get a new baby that worked. He said that his daddy took any car he had that didn't work back to the shop. They either fixed it or they gave him a new one. We took him to the nursery and he was amazed – even more so when we told him he was as little as them, but he grew up and so would the new baby." We brought him home and he eagerly watched Fred grow up while we lived there.

Fred had a club foot when he was born. The doctor told me to exercise it three times a day. When he was 6 months old, his feet were put in special shoes attached to a rigid board to correct the club foot. Eventually he had special shoes fit with ankle braces. Now he is able to wear regular shoes with arch supports.

We went to live with George's parents when Fred was about 7 months old, then we moved several times. We lived in Cape May, New Jersey when George returned home from the service, then we moved to a small town near Richmond so that George could be closer to his father, who had had a stroke.

Up to this time Fred developed normally. While we were there, Fred got encephalitis, with a temperature of 105. The doctor warned us that if Fred survived, he would have severe brain damage. He remains mildly retarded to this day. We moved to Georgia then so that George could be released from the army.

We moved to Valparaiso so that George could teach at Valparaiso University. While there, Tom was born. Fred has always been an easy child to manage, wanting to please and thoughtful of others. Baby's crying upset him. He demanded that Mom respond immediately. The same after Linda and Martha were born.

Linda had blonde curly hair after she was born. Her hair changed markedly by the time she was ready for school (dark and straight).

Shortly after we moved to Janesville, George had to go back to teaching at Valparaiso because the goat farm had less than the promised income. I wrote of this in an earlier chapter. Because I also had to work to provide for our family, Grandma Peg was asked to come to help care for the children. When Peg left, both George and I were able to find employment in Janesville on different shifts so that between us we could care for the children.

When Linda was 6, Martha was born. Harry helped with the children for a time. In 1957 when I returned to nurses' training in order to become an RN, Granny Reuss came to stay with the family.

I have already described how God was with me during the unusual births of my children. God also provided individuals from my family who taught me and supported me during their infancy.

Growing up on the farm gave the children the opportunity to see God's work in creation together. The garden and fields and animals: breeding, birthing, nurturing, and dying showed them God's plan to survive for us as a family. They also learned responsibility to work with each other under the supervision of adults and eventually to function independently.

I have already described how God worked in our lives through St. Paul's and Faith Lutheran Churches. This faith sustains all of us to this day.

The children walked to Willowdale country school where Mrs. Klusmeyer was the teacher for grades 1-8. Children brought their own lunch each day. Occasionally the teacher provided hot soup warmed on the potbellied stove in the back of the room. The children worked together under her direction, helping all to learn.

Early in Linda's first year, Mrs. Klusmeyer called one day, laughing. She said we were studying Wisconsin 100 years ago, and your children said that their mother was 100 years old and they could prove it. How? Your braids were down to your hips, and it would take that long to grow braids that long. I told her that I had told the children of living in the hill country of West Virginia where some children did not have electricity or running water and used out-houses like people did 100 years ago.

Tom, Linda and Fred attended St. Paul's parochial school for a year. Fred was repeatedly knocked down on the playground. When George complained to the principal, he was told that Fred needed to learn to take care of himself on the playground. The kids went to a consolidated country school after that. One year of that was more than enough!

In eighth grade a test was given. Those who passed were admitted to middle school in Janesville. I had to intervene to see that Fred could attend because he did not pass the test. He needed to have written permission from the state and the county to be enrolled in the first special education class in the junior high school in Janesville. The county provided transportation. Fred then attended high school and graduated 3 years later.

We encouraged the children to participate in 4-H where they showed their projects at the Rock County Fair. They attended Lutherdale Bible Camp and scout camp.

Every year when we showed goats at the Wisconsin State Fair the children visited the fair. We took the children to outdoor movies and to swim at Lake Geneva. We took several trips "back east" to visit George's family and my father. We took them to see Grandma Peggy in California by train, and visited Tijuana in Mexico while there. We drove to Yellowstone Park and the Black Hills. We also saw Wisconsin attractions: Knott's Berry Farm, Cave of the Mounds, New Glarus, the Dells, and the cheese dairies in Monroe!

From 1958, I worked in public health, first as a nurse, then as assistant director and finally as director. During this time, I was organizing the community to meet the needs, so I was often gone in the evening for meetings. I also was on the board of the local association for retarded children and the national association for retarded children. This sometimes took me away on weekends. George was on his own for child care!

My biological children have asked that I tell about the years they spent at home, and tell only brief sketches of their lives after they left home, with the exception of Fred who had stayed with me to the present time. Tom entered his story, Linda wrote a brief story and so did Martha. I added some more information to each with their permission.

In the many decades up to the present, I have tried to be present for weddings, baptisms, confirmations and other events and celebrations of the family whenever I was invited. I have kept in touch on the phone and e-mail also. This is true for many of my foster children too.

Fred

I have described his early years in previous chapters. I do not remember if I told about Fred's special gift with bees. He was taught beekeeping by Mr. Meton. He was never stung and could move bees from one hive to another with his bare hands and arms. He once removed bees that escaped from their containers in the Post Office by himself. Then the farmers sprayed poison on the crops near us and killed his bees.

After Fred graduated from high school, he found employment in eight businesses. He washed dishes, filled orders for mixed grain, cleaned floors at body shops and grocery stores, used a machine to make meat patties and sorted materials at thrift stores. He was never fired, however in some cases the employer or supervisor ordered his to do a task which was dangerous for him, or illegal. On some of these occasions, he was injured. This necessitated back surgery twice and two brief hospitalizations. I had to intervene several times to help him learn to protect himself. Finally, he found safe employment at Goodwill in Janesville.

We moved to Arizona and he worked at Fry's grocery store. While there, he received employee of the month for each of the five years we lived there, so he received a special award when we left because they were still using the suggestions he had made. They also gave him a picnic because he had saved the life of another employee. We moved to Stoughton, Wisconsin, where he worked at Bethesda Thrift Store in nearby Madison. He was working there until two days before his last stroke in 2015.

When he was having his stroke, we were signing the documents for us to live together for the first time in an apartment in Stoughton. It was evident that this was God's plan so that I could take care him in his recovery!

He received the necessary therapies in Stoughton until we moved back to Arizona in 2016. We moved to Brookdale North Chandler, a facility that provides independent and assisted living as well as skilled nursing care. Our apartment is in independent living. We participate in the games and activities offered here.

Fred goes to Tempe Day Care three mornings a week, where he is in a special physical exercise group and practices communication skills. We attend Phoenix Church of Christ where he was baptized in January 2016 in Brookdale's pool. Plans have been made for his care if the time comes that I am not able to care for him.

Tom

Tom learned to do all the chores on the farm as he grew up. He helped Fred learn tasks as he needed and eventually became responsible for the other children when George and I were not there. He helped George with bottling the milk at Arbuthnot Dairy in Janesville after school when he was in high school.

Tom graduated from high school in 1964 and went to Wartburg College in Waverly Iowa. In 1967, he graduated and married Edee Dodd. He enrolled at Wartburg Seminary and graduated in 1971. He has served as pastor of congregations in Iowa until the present.

I briefly went to be with Tom and Edee to help take care of Edee, who had lupus, to teach others to manage her care which she needed for dialysis at home. She wrote and published a book called "Thus Far" about her experience with lupus. Edee died in 1979.

Tom and Edee's sons, Jon and Peter, stayed with us for a week or so during several summers. They went on some of our summer trips. Peter is a pastor in the ELCA now. Peter married Shannon and had Benjamin. After a long illness, Shannon died several years ago. We visited them at their home in Eyota, Minnesota and their cabin on the lake many times. Peter was married to Danielle Pearson on June 3rd, 2017, in Iowa. Peter's son Benjamin is in college now. Tom's son Jon has two children, Hannah and Aaron. Hannah is in college now and Aaron just graduated from high school.

Tom is now married to Ginny Bantz. Tom and Ginny have two children, Sarah and Jim. Sarah is a teacher. She married Landan Auld. They live in Marshalltown, Iowa. Jim is an engineer and works in Detroit, Michigan. He visited me here with Tom a few years ago.

Linda

As she grew up Linda took responsibility for feeding the chickens, rabbits, and baby goats as well as spending hours gardening, as we grew our own food. To this day, she has an aversion to spiders and their webs! She assumed many household chores, cooking cleaning, making school lunches and dinners and helping to can fruits and tomatoes. She had friends in the neighborhood and learned to detassel corn at twelve. This enabled her to earn nearly all of her college expenses. She learned to sew in 4-H and made most of her clothes in high school. She loved to sing and was in the choir at church. She even tried a couple of years of music lessons.

Linda attended Wartburg College with her brother, Tom, for two years as a social work major, having decided on this in 10th grade. She met her husband, Doug Hart, at Wartburg and dated him for three years before marrying him in Minneapolis, on March 14, 1969. She had graduated the night before from the University of Minnesota with honors. She had transferred to the University of Minnesota in 1967.

They moved to Missouri, where Doug was stationed in the army and then moved to Cedar Rapids in Iowa for Doug to complete his college education and for Linda to complete a Master's Degree in Social Work. Then they moved to Des Moines, Iowa, where their two children, Rachel (bid 8/20/75) and Benjamin (bid 1/6/79) were born. Linda worked in many social settings specializing in child, marriage and family therapy. while Doug worked in union organization. In 1989, they moved to Chicago where Linda worked in Child Protective Services and Doug became President of the local SEIU. They retired, and moved to Tempe Arizona to be near their daughter, Rachel and her husband Brandon Tarlowski who she had married in May 1998. They have two children Noah (bid 2/13/02) and Taryn (bid 12/22/06). Rachel divorced in 2011 and married Jason Anderson on June 21, 2014. They live close by in Chandler, Arizona, and visit frequently with all of us.

Since age eleven, Linda's relationship with God has been her foundation which has guided her in her choice of career – seen as her ministry in loving and care for others. God has most importantly guided her to see her need to repent make Jesus Lord of her life and be baptized as an adult by immersion to become a disciple of Jesus in the Chicago Church of Christ in 1996. She and Doug have both been biblically converted to Jesus and remain faithful in retirement. Their life has been very active in mentoring couples, counseling people and starting charity and senior organizations in their church and in the Phoenix and Tucson areas. They also take care of Fred and me by seeing that our needs are met.

We cherish our relationships with all of family! God has richly blessed us!

Martha

As the youngest of four children, Marty was blessed with many opportunities that her other siblings did not have. She had examples of successful behaviors to emulate and negative behaviors to avoid. She had the advantage of being able to play with neighbor children – a luxury her older siblings did not enjoy. With both parents working outside the home, she learned to work with her siblings to care for our farm animals, to tend gardens and to complete housework. Work was something that she learned to enjoy – setting time and quota goals for herself to accomplish tasks in a timely fashion so that she could finish and have time to play alone or with others.

She believes she and the rest of her siblings learned self-reliance as children. Work, good grades at school, and getting along with others was expected. Using time and resources wisely was taught and developed through home chores, church activities and 4-H. George and I invested in a CAP home for the children – a do it yourself house project – that gave us of them experiences in carpentry, drywalling, roofing, siding, and painting. It was an opportunity for George to teach them skills that they weren't aware their dad had. The finished home was something we were all proud of.

Martha was able to take piano lessons when she was six or seven and found that this was something that she really enjoyed. Her siblings quit taking lessons when they reached middle school, but

Marty was able to continue into high school and college. She feels that piano has been a blessing in her life and continues to bless others through teaching and sharing music in a variety of settings.

When she was in middle school, two of her siblings went off to college and we began taking in foster children. All but three of these children were younger than she, so she became their role model in the home. Active participation in our church youth group took her to a weekend outing in Milwaukee where she met her future husband, Tom. She was 15 and he was 17. Seven years later, after graduating from high school and college, they married and now have three grown children – Kaleb, Jacob and Esther. Kaleb and his wife, Hannah, have three children – Sylvan, Cosima and Nell. Esther and her husband, Aaron have two daughters – Gwendolyn and Rowan.

Tom is currently retired. He enjoys music, travelling, singing in the church choir and cooking. Marty teaches piano, Sunday School, directs her church choir, and sells Mary Kay. They both enjoy Bible studies and look forward to being reunited with all of our extended families in heaven when this earthly journey is over.

Noah's Ark Trip

Martha took me to the Creation Museum in Kentucky by Answers in Genesis many years ago – I thoroughly enjoyed it! In November 2018, she and Tom gave me the gift of a trip to see the replica of Noah's Ark built in Kentucky by Answers in Genesis. She planned the trip.

I flew to Ft. Wayne, Indiana, to visit with my foster daughter, Barbara Burnett, and her family. Another foster daughter Chris McCarthy was visiting there. She is a nursing assistant and offered to help me for the trip. The next day we drove to the Ark. We spent four hours there experiencing the wonderful exhibits and films that showed that God had shown Noah exactly how many cubits it took for length, width and height! A cubit is the distance between the tip of your finger and the tip of your elbow! The films explained how God planned to provide everything needed for the survival of all the plants and animals on the Ark for a long time. We saw the interesting display of the "kinds" of animals God created that have evolved into the kinds of animals we have today. Noah's family living quarters were on the top (third floor) deck, reached by a ramp that served all floors. There are no steps in the Ark.

I bought two DVDs, one about the planning and building of the Ark and the second about the exhibits and films. I plan to share them with my facility, Fred's day care and my church.

The next day, Barb drove Chris and me to Janesville where we stayed at a hotel that arranged a place for us to visit with friends. We visited all day and evening with many foster families, including some from Ft. Atkinson. The next day we drove to Stoughton where I had lived for many years. We visited with friends at the Senior Center where I had volunteered and saw friends from church, too. Then we drove to Skaalen Home where I had worked for many years until I retired. We had supper with Pastor Lund, a longtime friend and resident there, Pastor Todd from Good Shepherd

Lutheran Church, who had baptized me, my son Tom and his wife Ginny, my daughter Marty and her husband Tom, and David Hondt, an evangelist friend – all of whom I had not seen for many years! What a perfect way to end a fabulous trip!

I flew home from Rockford the next day. God gave me a wonderful trip to enjoy!

In Conclusion

My journey with God began with the first prayer I learned from my grandfather:

> Now I lay me down to sleep.
>
> I pray Thee Lord my soul to keep.
>
> If I should die before I wake,
>
> I pray Thee Lord my soul to take.
>
> If I should live for other days,
>
> I pray thee Lord to guide my ways.

My grandfather Lee taught me that God had made me and he called Him Lord sometimes. He said God put a soul in me that would help me be good and that I would go to heaven when I died. I say this prayer every night.

The next lesson I learned was about death when I was five. My Great Grandpa Springsteen lived with my Grandfather and Grandma Lee. I had been sent to call Great Grandpa Springsteen to breakfast one morning. I loved him. He had been caring for me since I was four because my brother Jim had polio and grandma and grandfather needed to care for Jim. Great Grampa Springsteen had taught me reading, writing, and arithmetic and told me stories – I loved him.

He was lying in bed with the tiny overhead light on – his eyes were closed, his Bible open on his chest, his glasses folded in his hands – He had died in his sleep.

The funeral was in the living room – I climbed on a chair, kissed his cheek and said, "Goodbye." I watched the coffin be closed, went to the cemetery and saw him buried. I prayed that night. When I came to "If I should die before I wake" I was terrified and cried, "I don't want to go to heaven now!" Grandpa Lee held me on his lap and comforted me. "God has many good things planned for you to do before He calls you to heaven. Great Grandpa was 94 years old and had done many good things. He was tired, so God took him to heaven where he is happy now. You have a long time before God takes you to be happy in heaven with Him." Lesson learned!

When I was six, I moved to Hagerstown with my parents for the first time. I learned about Jesus and more about God when I was given permission to follow some children to Sunday School. I got my first Bible from a Sunday School teacher there.

The next lasting experience was the tramp "angel" who rescued Jim and me from the tank car. We had banged "Save Our Souls" with the broken ladder rung on the tank wall. We were sure and still believe that he was sent to rescue us. And that God loved us. Throughout our lives ever after we knew God would be with us. He has been as I recounted the many times He saved my life. He arranged many "coincidences" that reminded me of His presence.

He taught me to forgive even people who harmed me and showed me how to love others. I learned that the test of faith is in works, not words or the church you go to.

I lived with families who went to five different Christian churches and two families who did not go to church at all (my parents and grandparents). Most followed Scripture. My parents did not until they were older – my father came back to faith in his 60's and my mother came to faith in Christ for the first time before she died. Two Jewish families followed the Old Testament. One of these families fed us for a week before our father abandoned us at the home of a former neighbor in West Virginia. The other Jewish family helped me understand my grandma's grief after grandpa's death. They also gave her free legal help with problems she had with his estate. A Christian black lady taught me to "talk to God whenever I needed to." She showed me love through hugs, many kindnesses and understanding when I needed it as a teenager.

In my journey with God I was able to view much of His creation: In the heavens I saw the aurora borealis, falling stars, eclipses of the sun and moon. I saw His mighty power in two tornados, one downdraft and a hurricane.

On Earth I worked in a flood, survived in a huge wave that was caused by an earthquake at sea, felt two small earthquakes. I saw a volcano, swamps, mountains, gorges, deserts, forests, farm lands, springs, rivers, waterfalls, lakes and two oceans.

Then God gave the gift of life to the plants, trees, microorganisms, insects, birds, animals, and last of all to man so that all His creation could work together to maintain the earth He created. I saw evidence of this working together that benefitted me everywhere I looked! Trees gave me oxygen, I gave them carbon dioxide, plants gave me food and medicine, bees gave me food, worms made the ground more fertile and provided food for fish. In my personal life, dogs rescued two children, a horse rescued a neighbor, birds and squirrels warned me of a wolf in Alaska. I read about porpoises rescuing people in the ocean. After the oil spill in the Gulf of Mexico, I read that people have discovered microorganisms that digest the oil that spilled and that seeps from the ocean floor all the time. They make the ocean safe for the fish! These were just a few of the examples I saw of God's creation working together!

Writing my journey with God has allowed me to learn to appreciate His creation more fully and to appreciate the many people who witnessed to me by teaching me about God and Jesus, introducing me to the Bible, and by loving and nurturing me so that I came to love God and acknowledge my sins, repent, be baptized, and accept the salvation offered by Jesus so that I can be in Heaven someday. I must obey Him and witness for Him the rest of my life.

- Mary Lee Reuss

www.ingramcontent.com/pod-product-compliance
Lightning Source LLC
Chambersburg PA
CBHW022216090526
44584CB00012BB/583